Get Your Happy Back

7 Principles to Get Unstuck and Take Back Your Power!

Diamond Leone

ISBN 978-0-5783-6685-2
eISBN 978-0-5783-6686-9

Copyright © 2022 by Diamond Leone

All rights reserved, including the right of reproduction in any form, or by any mechanical or electronic means including photocopying or recording, or by any information storage or retrieval system, in whole or in part in any form, and in any case not without the written permission of the author and publisher.

Published June 2022

Dedication

This book is dedicated to my mom, Lorna. She had the most incredible heart for God, the most amazing work ethic, and the most obnoxious, but infectious, laugh that I miss so dearly. "Love many, trust few, always paddle your own canoe," she would say. I love you and miss you beyond words.

To Brandon and Lauryn, my two precious gifts from God himself. You bring me more love and joy than I could have ever hoped for! May you always know how deeply loved you are. Please remember these three things:

- Always put God first and the rest will fall into place
- Protect and look out for each other and the rest of our family
- Remember to laugh at life, there's so much funny in it. And whatever you do, get out and see the world!

I love you with every cell in my body. Being your mom will forever be my greatest reward in life.

INTRODUCTION

> *Challenges are gifts that force us to search for a new center of gravity. Don't fight them. Just find a new way to stand*
>
> ~ Oprah Winfrey

Who is this book for?

This book is for you if you feel as if you have fallen off the path of happiness and are ready for a significant mental shift. You are finally ready to roll up your sleeves and do the work to create and build a life that is more intentional and purposeful.

Life is constantly being redefined for us, sometimes not on our terms. Before we realize it, happiness seems to slip away little by little, until we wake up one day and feel that we have no happiness left, or even worse, we don't remember who we are anymore.

Maybe you've suffered through a painful breakup or divorce that left you hurting and you have no idea how to bounce back. Maybe you come from a childhood that was riddled with uncertainty and dysfunction which could have played a role in emotionally holding you back over the years. Perhaps you have lost a loved one, had health issues, undergone financial crises, or maybe this recent pandemic has wreaked havoc in your life that you feel no one can possibly understand.

Any one of the above things can leave us feeling directionless and lost. Some of you may have had more than one of these unfortunate events happen in your life.

It could also be that you are simply tired of floating through life without any real clarity as to what is possible for you. Maybe you don't know how to pull yourself out of mediocrity, but you do know for sure that you want to learn how to live more intentionally and focus on something bigger and bolder for yourself.

How can this book help you?

Just about every one of us has an area of our life that we are struggling in. You are not born knowing how to solve all the problems that come your way. I wrote this book because I have experienced and overcame many hurdles in my life using the strategies and tips included here! These proven practices have helped me and countless others over the years. If you show up with the willingness to be open to the principles in this book it can truly help you to regain clarity and control over your life.

Principles like:

- **Turn your past into your power** - how to use painful events from your past as fuel to push you forward

- **Expand your awareness** - Learning how our thoughts work, how to harness the power of self-love, and how setting even the smallest goals create happiness for us

- **Create your mental tool kit** - Creating an empowered mindset, employing the technique of visualization, and developing a system to destroy fear and self-doubt

- **Form amazing habits** - Understanding that repetition is the key to mastery, the power of accountability, and shattering old belief systems

- **Learn to pivot** - How to be open to change, find your passion, and reinvent yourself after major life changes

- **Level up** - Why it's important to develop key relationships, stop playing small, and reach back to help others

- **Get your happy back!** - Empower yourself to make your health a priority, your happiness must be intentional, and remember no matter how hard it gets, YOU'VE GOT THIS!

What I want for you

I want to help you put new tools in your mental tool kit to help you fight every negative emotion that creeps up. Self-doubt won't stand a chance once you learn how to use your mind properly to develop and put the right systems in place.

I want you to learn that real happiness is not a surface level, fleeting moment that you may have misunderstood it to be. True happiness comes from being connected to your core values, having a purpose filled life, and understanding your self ideal and who you are capable of becoming. There is a certain type of hope that you must always cultivate from within which gives you something bigger than yourself that you are working towards.

After reading this book you will feel inspired and empowered! No matter what you are going through in your life, I want you to know that you are not alone. The important thing is to not look back at your past and all the mistakes that you think you've made, but rather look at your future! Look at the promising things that will manifest in your life once you take a disciplined approach and do the inner work. These principles are easy to apply and will help you achieve more than you ever thought possible.

It's time to live life on your terms again! It's time to GET YOUR HAPPY BACK!

TABLE OF CONTENTS

PRINCIPLE 1
TURN YOUR PAST INTO YOUR POWER

CHAPTER ONE
All painful roads lead to growth — 3

CHAPTER TWO
Remember the good — 11

CHAPTER THREE
Using forgiveness to get unstuck — 19

PRINCIPLE 2
EXPAND YOUR AWARENESS

CHAPTER FOUR
Using your thoughts as leverage — 27

CHAPTER FIVE
Self-love mastery — 35

CHAPTER SIX
Defining your core values — 41

PRINCIPLE 3
CREATE YOUR MENTAL TOOL KIT

CHAPTER SEVEN
Determine your true goals 51

CHAPTER EIGHT
Mindset matters 57

CHAPTER NINE
Using the power of visualization 65

PRINCIPLE 4
FORM AMAZING HABITS

CHAPTER TEN
The art of reframing your story 71

CHAPTER ELEVEN
Putting the right systems in place 81

CHAPTER TWELVE
Creating killer habits 87

CHAPTER THIRTEEN (Bonus Chapter)
How to pull yourself out of a rut 93

PRINCIPLE 5
LEARN TO PIVOT

CHAPTER FOURTEEN
Be open to change 103

CHAPTER FIFTEEN
Finding your purpose or passion 109

CHAPTER SIXTEEN
Reinventing yourself after life's curve balls ... 115

PRINCIPLE 6
LEVEL UP

CHAPTER SEVENTEEN
Develop key relationships — 127

CHAPTER EIGHTEEN
Stop playing small — 133

CHAPTER NINETEEN
Reach back to help others — 139

PRINCIPLE 7
GET YOUR HAPPY BACK

CHAPTER TWENTY
Make your health a priority — 147

CHAPTER TWENTY-ONE
Happiness is intentional — 155

CHAPTER TWENTY-TWO
You've got this! — 161

Acknowledgements

Brandon and Lauryn - Being your mother has allowed me access to the greatest portal of love I've ever known. I'm so proud of the adults that you have grown and matured into. Know that I miss having our family meals together, driving you back and forth to school as we told funny stories and listened to Elton John. You guys make life worth living. I love you forever, I like you for always. As long as I'm living, my babies you'll be. May the knowledge and experience in this book continue to enlighten our family lineage long after I'm gone.

Cecil - Your love and support all these years means more than you'll ever know. Without you, so many things would not be possible. I love you to the moon and back.

Lael and Dawn - You were my original guardian angels. God knew to sandwich me neatly between the two of you in the birthing order. Thank you for being the best brother and sister all these years, I love you.

Laurie - I looked up "best friend for life" in the dictionary and there was a picture of you right there, I saw it with my own eyes. Your support and love all these years has been priceless. I'm so lucky to have your friendship. Love you always.

Many thanks to:

Victor - my muse during the first draft many years ago, conspirator, friend, and creative partner

Eric Whittleton - my very first beta reader, you really helped to shape this book to what it eventually became. Thank you so much!

Audrey Hoisington - my publishing bff. You were so gracious to hold my hand as I walked blindly into the world of publishing. I can't thank you enough.

Principle #1
Turn Your Past Into Your Power

In this Principle, we will be discussing how to use your past as leverage!

- ◆ All painful roads lead to growth

- ◆ Nothing lasts forever

- ◆ Using forgiveness to get unstuck

LET'S GET STARTED!

Chapter One
All Painful Roads Lead To Growth

Let's talk

I hated my childhood. We were really poor. Oh, and also I was tall, skinny, and awkward looking, and yet there I was, riding on a school bus with a bunch of other kids who also happened to be poor, but better off than I was. They were making fun of some unfortunate soul who had just been evicted from their home. I heard them yelling out, "Awwww look, yo! Somebody got put out!" Just as I turned my head to look out the window to see what all the fuss was about, I realized that the bus had turned onto the street where I lived. I remember this day like it was yesterday.

There was a group of people pilfering through someone's belongings that had been removed from the home and placed on the curbside. That's when I noticed someone carrying my mattress on their head down the street. Yep, those people who got evicted... that was our family. I made my way off the school bus fighting through the feelings of embarrassment, shame, and shock. Looking back, I don't remember wanting to cry. Instead, I felt like I needed to somehow find a solution, but felt powerless. It felt like I was inside of a really bad dream. I was 11 years old.

This is one of the many memories that shaped my childhood. Another thing I remember was that I asked a lot of questions. I thought that maybe if I kept asking questions, someone would be able to give me an answer that could make all the crappy stuff going on in my childhood make sense. The answers never came.

My mother was a single mom raising three kids on her own. In the evening hours, she was a dog trainer and during the daytime, she was a home improvement contractor and an aspiring real estate investor. She worked so hard to provide for us, but despite her best efforts, we went to bed hungry many nights and ended up being homeless quite often.

My mom used to love taking extended hot baths. She preferred the relaxed soaking of a bath over showers. She worked long hours and after her bath was over, she would quickly pass out asleep within minutes. My mom never sat still for long. She was either working or sleeping. So, the only time we really got to spend with her was while she was taking her bath. This was our family time. This may seem unusual to you but not to our little dysfunctional family. It was not uncommon for my mom to change her clothes or use the bathroom in front of us. She was very different than most other mothers. She treated us like adults in most ways. When my friends were curious about the topic of sex or trying to figure out what certain vernacular meant, I knew that I could simply go and ask my mom. I can still hear her now, "Oh that means a blow job, honey," as she would belt out laughter. My friends thought I had the coolest mom. In a lot of ways, I did.

She openly answered any questions about sex and nothing seemed taboo. She was very matter-of-fact and comfortable to talk to us about grown-up topics, and she usually did so from the bathtub. Having a private, parked seat on the toilet lid as I got to talk to my mom and have her undivided attention was the best feeling in the world! I can still remember the excitement when it was my turn to go in. The bathroom was so small that we each had to take turns going in there, and we had a very limited amount of time that was strictly enforced by the next sibling waiting. She would tell us stories of her day, how she worked on a house and the home improvement repairs that she learned and figured out on her own. Things like finding a better way to apply caulking, how to paint a wall using the roller from heel to toe so you don't leave streaks. Huh? Oh yes, she was very methodical and detail-oriented when she was teaching us a new skill. She would say "listen carefully because tomorrow I'm going to show you how to do this." More about our child slave labor later in this book.

When it was my turn to have my mother's ear, I would almost always ask about my dad. Have you seen him? I'd ask with such hope in my little voice. The answer was always no. My brother, sister and I all have different fathers. When I got old enough to understand the promiscuous reputation associated with having three kids by different fathers all one year apart, it was one more thing to add to the list of things that I would be embarrassed about growing up. She was unconventional in so many ways and someone I deeply loved but also was terrified of. My mother was very laid back and nonchalant about the things that most parents got upset about. Things like staying out late, drugs, smoking, sex, or even who you dated were no big deal to her. However, if you swept the floor and didn't complete the task by picking up the pile of dirt, or you were goofing off when she was trying to teach you something, or if you didn't fully complete a job that she assigned to you; that would send her through the roof.

My father was an industrial plumber who operated heavy machinery and installed big pipes underground. He also did domestic plumbing jobs as well. Since Mom and him were both in the home improvement circles, I always hoped they would run into each other, fall back in love, and we could all live happily ever after. As I sat next to the tub and processed that she still hadn't heard from or seen my dad, the tears began to well up in my eyes. When she saw how much I was missing my daddy again, she attempted to redirect my sadness by reminding me that I have his nose. "You know what else," she'd say. "Your laugh sounds exactly like his." Really? I'd say, as I started to perk up. In that moment, I felt comforted in the innocent assumption that if my laugh and my nose were exactly like his, there would be no denying that I was his daughter. No denying that I belonged to him. No denying that he was my father and supposed to love me. It made me feel justified to want and desperately seek out his love. It made my relation to him feel real, even if I had never met him.

As a little girl, I remember the pain in my heart of not feeling wanted by my dad. No one ever told me that he didn't want to be my father, but I felt it by his absence. If he only knew how much I needed and loved him, then maybe he wouldn't stay away. I dreamt of the day that I would meet this mysterious man who held my fragile little heart in his hands. In my perfect imaginary world, he would take one glimpse of the daughter he pretended not to know and wrap his protective arms around me, and love me unconditionally like a father is supposed to. That moment never came.

> *"Difficult roads often lead to beautiful destinations."*
> ~ Zig Ziglar

Lessons learned

Life can throw curve balls so fast that you don't have time to catch your breath before another one comes along. And yes, those fastballs are painful, but it's the slow curve balls, like the ones in my childhood, that really threw me for a loop. The slow, painful burn of coming to the realization that my father, the one man who is supposed to love me and protect me, ended up being the first man to ever break my heart by abandoning me.

I learned that as painful as it was to have experienced this type of rejection so early on in life, it taught me that people are fallible. People cannot give you what they don't have. They can be broken in the worst ways, and they cannot give you the love that you seek if they don't have it first to give to themselves.

I cried myself to sleep many nights because I felt like such a misfit in every way. I hated my appearance, and I hated my life; an outcast that wasn't loved. My family didn't look or feel like everyone else's. My childhood felt like a bad movie, and I was the main character trying to fumble my way through without a script. The pervasive feeling throughout my childhood was that of being constantly lonely. My mother was not like other moms. Although once strikingly beautiful in her younger years, she was odd, overweight, had an obnoxious laugh, and was self-employed. Nothing about her was feminine or dainty, not what society would consider gentle and mom-like. She wore wallaby shoes and muumuu outfits that she sewed together herself. She was definitely a misfit who didn't give two craps what anyone thought of her. Interestingly enough, she had the most positive outlook on life. Even though she was broke most of the time, I never heard her complain.

Using your setback as a set up

My mother was the most positive person you could imagine. It's because of her quiet strength that I learned to not be a complainer. She had a huge heart for wanting to help other people, as she did on many occasions. As messed up as some of her decision making was, she got a lot of things right. She led by example on the most important life lessons. She had a happy spirit and always wanted those around her to be happy too, which is why I felt called to write this book and share some of these stories and lessons in her honor. I've learned that every setback can be an opportunity for an amazing setup if you let it.

In life, we are unknowingly taught to have compassion usually from being in situations where we need someone to first show compassion to us. On the outset, someone could look at my childhood and say, "Wow, what a sad story". But you know what? This might surprise you, but I would not change a thing. If I could go back and rewrite my entire story, I would let everything happen the same way all over again.

Receiving food from generous people when I was a kid taught me to be generous to strangers who might be struggling. Being poor taught me to work hard and to save my money. Being homeless gave me the desire to later become a real estate investor and own many homes. Being left alone as a little kid for days at a time taught me to place a huge priority on family time with my own kids. I'm always looking for ways to give back. My eyes can see, and my heart can feel the pain of people who are struggling because I've been there. It is not what happens to you. It's what you do with what happens to you that defines who you become.

You can do hard things

Constantly yearning for the acknowledgement, love, and affection from a father who wouldn't give it to me was hard. It taught me to be emotionally resilient and strong. I learned that true love and acceptance comes from my Heavenly Father. He is the one who created me and loved me before I was born. Maybe you had a similar rejection from a parent in your early life. If you did, I know firsthand how much that sucks. But if you look closely, I bet there are some strengths that were created out of that pain. I believe we are all called to turn our pain into purpose, and when we do, our suffering becomes a guiding light to help others. This light can only be powered by the pain and the lessons from your journey. I want you to know that you can become a courageous warrior when you can look at life through this lens. Your painful experiences are a badge of honor that you can wear proudly because you did not let it break you.

Learning to forgive even when someone doesn't deserve it is hard. But you can do hard things. The quiet strength of forgiveness can be your superpower because it's extremely liberating to focus your energy and intentions on the life you are meant to live as opposed to spending that energy having resentment and anger over the life that never was. This life chose you, and you have an amazing opportunity to make the best of it.

And lastly, I learned that how you feel is not the result of what is happening to you, but rather your interpretation of it.

I don't want to simplify your pain or your experiences. I do, however, encourage you to examine the story that you may have told yourself around the unfortunate events. I want you to know that you get to decide the type of person you become as a result. These things are happening *for* you and not *to* you. Like mine, all of your painful roads can lead to the most amazing transformation in your life!

Chapter Two
Remember The Good

Let's talk

The day came where I finally got to meet my father. My mom said she ran into him on a jobsite and to hurry and get dressed if I wanted to go meet him because she was leaving in ten minutes. I don't think I have ever gotten dressed so fast in my entire life.

I remember feeling panicked, rushing so she wouldn't leave without me. This was the meeting of a lifetime. Nothing, and I mean nothing, was more important to me than this. He was this mystical figure that I had been dreaming of for as long as I could remember. He was the love of my life, my everything, and I needed to look presentable. I quickly reviewed all possible clothing options and suffice it to say everything I owned was crap. I had no pretty dresses to wear. Screw it, I thought. Time was wasting, and I didn't want to miss this big opportunity. I threw on the best of my raggedy clothes and ran to the car.

"There's your daddy!" My mom pointed out as we drove up to a job site. I saw an older white man sitting on top of a Caterpillar backhoe excavator. I'll never forget the moment I was close enough to see his face. I've never met Jesus in person, but I'm sure it would feel similar. Up to this point, I had never loved anyone more than this mystery man. I was so nervous! It felt like the first day of school when you show up and just hope and pray the other kids like you. But this feeling was deeper than that. I wanted my dad to choose me. To accept me. I wanted him to love me. My mom held my little hand as we walked up to this mammoth piece of machinery. I stretched my neck way up to the sky to see my dad sitting up high in the seat. Our eyes met, and I couldn't look away. I was filled with nerves, and my mouth wouldn't work. I forgot all of my words. This was the moment I had been waiting for my whole life. He looked down at me and sarcastically asked, "Who are you"?

My mom laughed, and the man sitting on top of this big machine laughed. I guess this was funny.

I didn't understand sarcasm. Hearing him ask who I was didn't seem funny at all. It felt cold, distant, and out of place for a father meeting his daughter for the first time. My mom said, "This is your daughter," interrupting the awkward moment. He replied, "Is that right?" He invited me to climb up to sit on his lap. He asked me what grade I was in, what was my favorite color. I remember thinking, "Can we talk about something more substantial, like where you've been for the last 11 years of my life? Did you miss me? Are you going to leave again?" The experience felt watered down and fake, but I was innocently still hopeful.

I didn't want to exchange meaningless pleasantries with the man I had been waiting for my whole life. I wanted to have a real conversation. I may have only been 11 years old, but I knew I wanted a meaningful conversation with him. He wanted to tell stories that had nothing to do with me or my mom. He told a story about a job he recently did, then another about the different types of equipment he could operate. It was like he wanted to stay on surface level. Every time I'd say something serious like, "I miss you, Dad", he replied with another question like, "Do you like school?" Each deflected reply stung with rejection. I was confused and trying to process things. I sat quietly and listened to his stories. It felt like the monthly adoption day at Pet Smart, and I was the cute little puppy hoping to be chosen. Finally, I worked up the courage to ask him if he could please come live with us, so I didn't have to miss him anymore. He laughed at my question and said that life wasn't that simple. Once again, I didn't understand his awkward humor.

The visit was rushed after my last question. Suddenly, he had to get back to work. My mom asked him if he could help out with buying some school clothes because she didn't have the money and the start of school was approaching. He said yes and helped me down off the machine. I didn't want to leave, but I didn't feel welcomed to stay. It was such a gut wrenching feeling that I had never felt before. If you mix disappointment, sadness, sorrow, and rejection, that's how it felt as we drove away.

As I wrote this chapter, I wrestled with which story I could share to really encapsulate one of the saddest and yet most life changing moments. I wish I could tell you that when all this happened, that I was strong and resilient and that none of it bothered me. I wish I could tell you that I knew everything would be okay and that God loved me and had a plan for my life. What I can tell you is that I felt so unloved. I was rejected to my core. There is a saying, "more is caught than taught" when raising children. On that day, I "caught" that my father was not interested in knowing me, let alone loving me.

> *Always remember the proverb: "This too shall pass." Your feelings won't last forever, there's a light at the end of every tunnel. It might not happen today or tomorrow, but you'll feel better eventually.*
> ~Paulo Coelho

Lessons learned

I've learned that nobody gets through life unscathed. I'd be lying if I told you that I've gotten over my father's rejection. There are some things in life that you never quite "get over," but you can learn how to manage the power that they have. You are made up of more than your emotions and feelings. You have an amazing mind that is unbelievably powerful, and you can learn skills to train it to be your biggest ally when pain tries to defeat you.

Our brains are designed to tell us a story that gives meaning to each thing that happens to us. If we do not intentionally narrate an empowering story, our minds will, by default, create one that can be negative, defeating, and self-sabotaging. You can learn to change the story you tell yourself by using a technique called *reframing*. For example, in my case, I used to believe that I was unlovable because I had a parent who rejected me. I changed my story to a more empowered one where I tell myself that I am lovable, that I am worthy, and that I am made with love from my heavenly Father. My new story tells me that my earthly father could not give me what he didn't have and it was a blessing that I was not raised by him at all. You get to decide how much power these memories have over you. You can also choose to take away their power by telling yourself a better and more empowering story. There are several other things you can use to help come to terms with painful memories, like counseling, inner self work/coaching, and prayer. I have done all these, and I use them in addition to the technique of reframing, which we will talk more about later.

Maybe you had two loving parents who made you feel secure and emotionally safe, so feeling unloved in your childhood wasn't your cross to bear. However, today you are going through a terrible breakup that has left you feeling isolated and empty. Maybe you are going through a health or financial crisis, and no matter what you do, you can't seem to find level ground. Although these things come into our life and try to render us powerless, the truth is we have the power to decide how these events will affect us. First and foremost, you are not your feelings. As mentioned in Chapter 1, how you feel is not the result of what is happening in your life but rather your interpretation of what is happening. It's important to make this distinction because it gives you the opportunity to choose how you will proceed. You don't have to settle for the role of a victim.

Nothing lasts forever

Here's what I know: life can be very unfair. You are a good person, and although I may not know you personally, I know that you are worthy of happiness. If you are going through a tough time right now, I want you to take a moment and breathe. Take another big deep breath if you need to, and know that even though it feels bad right now, things do and will get better. They say that nothing good lasts forever, but you know what? Nothing bad lasts forever, either. That's because nothing in itself lasts forever, not even you or me. This is all a temporary journey. We are passing through life, and if we can accept this as fact, maybe we would be less likely to let circumstances, people, or events steal our joy.

You are so much stronger than you know

The other important point I want you to know is that growth can only happen through pain. You grow through what you go through. If you are a spiritual person, have you considered that maybe God/the universe has something amazing for you to do in this lifetime? However, in order for you to do that amazing assignment, you might first need to be developed in certain areas. It's not until we get on the other side of pain and discomfort that we realize what our lessons are. It helps to frame each painful experience with the knowledge that something good will eventually come from it. Even if that something is that we become more resilient for the next challenge for which we are faced.

That being said, I do not want you to think that you have to sit in misery and pain as these things are unfolding in your life. You get to decide how long you stay in a state of suffering. Sometimes, we can't control our external forces, but we can control our internal forces. Things like our attitude, our perspective, our energy, and the time that we allow ourselves to spend ruminating on what has happened to us. These all play a huge role in our ability to heal and bounce back after a setback.

Being proactive about your joy takes work and being intentional. You don't have to sit around and be sad every day because you are going through a difficult time in your life. Trust me on this; I have been in the middle of painful experiences in my life and still decided to wake up and choose joy. During that chaos, I learned to have peace, and you can too. Not every day will be smooth sailing, of course; some days will be better than others. Take a deep breath on the difficult days. It's okay to cry when you need to. Be patient with yourself and the process. When you adopt the mindset that you are not going to allow yourself to stay in a state of despair for very long, your outer world changes. You are creating space for a magical shift. Your focus changes to things that bring you joy. You start to give yourself something fun and exciting to look forward to each day.

I realized something about life a long time ago, and maybe it can help you. I learned that it is difficult for us to let go of a job, a belief, a relationship, or a situation that isn't fulfilling if we don't feel we have something better to move towards. If you are in the middle of a stressful situation, start thinking about something enjoyable you'd like to move towards. Whatever you are going through now will not last forever and will eventually become the past.

Chapter Three
Using Forgiveness To Get Unstuck

Let's talk

They say that not forgiving someone is like drinking poison and hoping the other person dies. My father eventually made his way over to our home with some school clothes for me. It was his only contribution to my childhood. I was excited that he was bringing them for me. It wasn't even about the clothes; I just really wanted to see my dad again.

For hours, I waited for him to arrive. It was getting late when I asked my mom what time it was, and she said it was after 11PM. It felt like an eternity as I kept looking out the window each time I heard the sound of a car passing by. My eyelids were getting heavy, and I eventually fell asleep. The next morning, I ran to my mom with excitement. "Did dad drop off my school clothes?" I asked, with the anticipation of a kid on Christmas morning. My mom pointed to a brown paper bag sitting in the corner. It was wrinkled and had been rolled halfway down. "It's in that bag," she said in a flat voice. I remember that her tone sounded off and unhappy.

I ran over, unrolled the top of the bag and dug in with anticipation. What I found in there would take years of healing. (I am taking deep breaths as I write this.) Inside the bag was hand-me-down clothes that were well worn and obviosly used because one of the pants had worn out knees. I was confused. I asked my mom why would he bring someone's used clothing to me? She tried to casually explain that maybe his other daughter outgrew them and perhaps he was passing them down to me. Her tone and wording was likened to a Doctor telling you everything would be okay just before amputating your leg. It was not okay to me. I didn't know my father had other children. This topic was never brought up before and I guess I never thought to ask. Him having other children or bringing used clothing to his illegitimate kid may not seem like a big deal to some, but for me, these were devastating blows. Giving me hand me down clothing from a daughter that he was willing to purchase new clothes for and claim as part of his family made the rejection piercingly real that I didn't matter to him. That I was an outkast and an afterthought. Like those used clothes, I wasn't of any value.

The fantasy world that I spent years creating in my head, that my father would one day walk into my life and love me, came crashing down upon me. I burst into tears because my little heart could only take so much pain and disappointment at one time. My mother did the best she could to console me. But after she told me that he had another daughter and the realization he had given me her hand-me-down clothes, I mentally checked out. I went into full on hatred mode for my father. I wanted him to go back to being nonexistent. Knowing him hurt way more than not. I felt like such a fool for loving him all of those years. I became angry at myself for getting my hopes up so high and for wanting him to be a part of my life. I decided in that moment that the adults in my life were very disappointing.

I remember thinking that when I grow up, I am going to be so rich that I could buy myself whatever new clothes I wanted. I vowed I would *never* need to depend on him or anyone else ever again!

I know, I know, that was a bit dramatic, but I was 11-years-old, and I was a little extra even back then. Sadly, it wasn't even about the clothes. To know that he cared enough for his other daughter to buy her new clothes was one thing, but to turn around and give her used clothes as his only present to me was so hurtful and quite pathetic. It solidified the feelings I felt on the day I met him: he didn't care about me, he didn't value me, and he damn sure didn't love me. That was the last time I ever asked about my father. Keep in mind, this belief system and opinion of my father formed when I was 11 years old. It wasn't until I was well into adulthood that I unpacked all of these emotions and was able to change the story around them. I would also like to point out that I reconnected with my father later in life. It's a totally different experience to see someone through the lens of an empowered adult, versus that of a helpless child. You can stand on empathy and compassion versus resentment.

> "Forgiveness is giving up the hope that the past could have been any different."
> ~ Oprah Winfrey

Lessons learned

Life isn't supposed to be fair

I've learned over the years that life doesn't always give you what you deserve. You can do everything right and show up as the very best version of yourself in a career and still get fired. You can be the best husband or wife and still get cheated on. You can be the most amazing sacrificial parent and love your kids with all your heart only to have them choose the wrong path in life. Do you understand what I'm saying here? Life isn't meant to be fair. Life is meant to be navigated. The better equipped you are internally to manage your own mental state, the easier you can cope when life blindsides you, and make no mistake, it *will* blindside you from time to time.

Letting go is a superpower

I was the kid who was searching for love and acceptance. I wanted to feel like I belonged. I wanted to feel like I was wanted. I felt like I desperately needed attention and wanted somebody to look at me and say, "yes, you are worthy of love." My mom was absent a lot because she was a working, single mom. Since she was always gone, you can imagine how lonely I felt all of the time. As a child, I felt entitled to certain things like feeling loved, feeling emotionally safe, and to feel wanted by both of my parents. And for the record, I do think all kids should have these things. But when you hold onto a belief that you are entitled to something no matter what it is, your life can spiral out of control, leading you to cope in unhealthy ways if you don't receive it.

Since life doesn't deal a perfect hand to any of us, it is critically important that we learn how to best play the cards we are dealt.

As I got older, I looked for that love and acceptance in my relationships. It never came. I eventually learned to let go of the idea that my father or a partner owed me anything at all. I learned that in trading expectations for appreciation in life, I found a new type of freedom. I found a unique power within myself that I was in control of, and no one could take that power away from me. It is not someone else's job to make you happy or even to make you feel loved. The feeling of true love and acceptance must come from within yourself and your relationship with your Higher Power (God, Universe, etc.) And once you find this within yourself, you will naturally align with and attract supportive people.

Forgiveness equals freedom

Forgiveness is the only path to freedom from darkness. It is the path to becoming unstuck from your past. Forgiveness is giving up the hope that the past can be any different. None of us can go back and change anything from our past, so why do we hold on to anger, hurt feelings, or rage? Sometimes, it's because we feel it's our way of honoring our pain. We feel that if we hold onto the anger, it is a form of solidarity with our strength of having survived what happened to us. But what if *not forgiving* is a form of poison that we also carry within us that destroys our ability to feel alive, happy, or free? Forgiveness is accepting that it has already happened to you. It's letting go so the past does not hold you prisoner any longer. My life shifted tremendously when I started giving out forgiveness like candy. I started by forgiving my father years ago, and I have used forgiveness as a healing tool ever since. It has been the best form of healing in my life. I look at forgiveness like a stock on Wallstreet that pays dividends. There are certain stocks that when you buy them, they pay you a cash dividend each quarter. Meaning all you have to do is hold these stocks in your brokerage account, and you get paid just to have them in your portfolio. Forgiving is something that pays dividends for years. You are free to invest the rest of your time doing more constructive things rather than holding onto bitterness.

Voluminous people

Pastor TD Jakes said, "Sometimes your parents were broken when you got them. There are people amongst us like you and me who are voluminous. We are 10-gallon people. We may have been born in families with people who have pint sized capacities. When you are a 10-gallon person and you want love, you want it for the same amount. But a pint-sized person could be sincerely giving you all they have. But it doesn't fill you up because you're bigger than that, but you must realize that with some people, that's all they've got."

Maybe you are a voluminous person, and you have a huge capacity to love, to show compassion, and to nurture another human being. And because of your huge heart, you can't see how or why someone could hurt you in the ways that they did. It's not your job to analyze why or how someone could hurt you because when we try to understand the situation, we become stuck in a loop of despair. Sometimes there are no answers as to why something has happened. At some point, we have to decide: do we want answers, or do we want healing? But often times, we can't have both.

Principle #2
Expand Your Awareness

In this principle, we are peeling back the layers to discover who you are and what you really want out of life!

- Using your thoughts as leverage

- Self-love mastery

- Defining your core values

LET'S GET STARTED!

Chapter Four

Using Your Thoughts As Leverage

Let's talk

In Principle 1, we talked about how to turn our past disappointments and pain into our power. I shared with you some of the ways that I was able to overcome the most painful moments of my childhood. And while there were many more over the course of my life, the magnitude of my father's rejection set the stage for years of low self-esteem, lack of self-worth, and decreased self-confidence.

Keep in mind that I had no idea there were vicious, destructive thoughts playing on a mental loop and would be the foundation that I stood on when making every decision in my life. The jobs and the amount of pay I would settle for, the poor friendships I would put up with, and the type of men I ended up dating were all byproducts of the decisions I made that were using a broken computer spitting out faulty data.

In Principle 2, I want to take you on a journey to share with you some of the insights that I learned and how I was able to expand my awareness to reprogram my thoughts to better serve me.

When I was in my early thirties, my marriage ended, and I felt like an utter failure. A failure because the dream of giving my kids the family unit that my parents couldn't give me was dying. I had two small children, and since I had given up my career in the computer field years earlier to raise them, I was unemployed. I had recently secured my real estate license but up to that point, I had only dabbled in real estate part-time. I didn't have enough skills or experience in this new field to rely on as a primary source of income. I was terrified about what our future would look like. If you've ever gone through a divorce with little kids in tow, it's the equivalent of going through a war zone, and while you are trying to protect yourself and figure out what the future holds, you're also desperately trying to minimize any emotional casualties for your family. The reason I am sharing this is that besides the power of my prayers, there was only one thing that saved me: my thoughts. Every day, I fought hard to keep the right perspective by flooding my mind with gratitude, empowerment, and the right people who supported this new chapter in my life. Failure was not an option!

I also made it a point to cut off any people who made me feel small. I refused to be around negative or judgmental people. This meant letting go of some so-called friendships. As ugly as divorce can be, I was determined to come out of it with as much of a winning scenario for my entire family (and yes, that included my soon to be ex-husband) as possible. And so, I did. But it all began with committing my thoughts to the desired outcome.

Lessons learned:
Understanding how our thoughts work

When I realized that our thoughts are energy, it was a game changer. What if I told you that where you are right now in your life is a direct reflection of the type of thoughts you have and the energy that surrounds them?

You need to pay attention to the thoughts that you have throughout your day. Here's how it works: We are vibrational beings that give and respond to energy. Each one of our thoughts produces energy, and with each thought, we actually send out energy into the world.

If you find yourself in a place of unhappiness in your life, like I was with my divorce, and you want to pull yourself out of an emotional hole, then you have to learn what a central role your thoughts play in every single thing that you do. Your thoughts control every area of your life because your thoughts have energy, and that same energy actually attracts or repels things to or from you.

In the book *The Secret* by Rhonda Byrne, she explains the law of attraction as a simple concept of like attracts like. Think of your thoughts like a big vibrational magnet. We all know how a magnet works, and similarly whatever thoughts you have, you are attracting more of that same vibrational energy back into your life. It's a vibrational pull that takes the energy around our thoughts and pushes similar outcomes back to us.

> *"Everything is energy. When you match the frequency of the reality that you want, you cannot help but get that reality. This is how energy works. It is not philosophy. This is physics."*
> ~ Rhonda Byrne, The Secret

Thoughts and their impact on relationships

We all bring baggage to a relationship. The key is to learn healthy ways to manage it so you don't unknowingly self-sabotage a healthy relationship. Sometimes the hardest thing to learn is how to navigate a perfectly good relationship after you have left a bad one. What do I mean? Let's say your last relationship was toxic. Maybe someone mistreated you, but you're single now and on the dating scene, looking for a new partner. If you are constantly worried about whether this new person might mistreat you in the same manner as your last relationship, you are subconsciously attracting the same type of relationship back into your life with your own thoughts! This is why some people find themselves dating the same type of person over and over. Yikes! No, thanks.

Now that you understand the power of your thoughts, do you see how your thoughts can play a huge role in how happy you feel? It's hard to be happy if you are predisposed to thinking the worst in every situation. What I want you to take away from this chapter is that you must think about what it is that you *do* want, not what you *don't* want. Think of a loving and emotionally safe relationship you want. Let yourself feel the warmth of this beautiful union. This is how you begin the process of manifesting what you want to have in your life. We will talk more about this concept of manifesting later when we discuss visualization.

Using your thoughts as leverage

At the beginning of this chapter, I shared with you how the rejection I experienced from my father created a vicious loop of negative thoughts that played in the background of my mental computer. These negative thoughts unknowingly caused me to suffer for many years with low self-esteem. As a result of this low self-esteem, certain decision-making processes were broken because it was using faulty data, meaning data that was not true at all.

Maybe you have areas of your life that are not where you want them to be because, like me, you have been using faulty data when making decisions in your own life. When you wake up to this realization, you might easily feel defeated because you don't know how to fix it. I believe the key to fixing a faulty decision-making process is to reverse engineer it by asking yourself the right questions to help you understand how you felt. Where was your mindset when you made the decisions that took you down a wrong path?

The answer to this question can be powerful, and you can use it as leverage to help you make better decisions moving forward. If you want things to change in your life, you have to change first. I have put together a list of questions below in some key areas of life that can help you get started with this process. By the way, maybe you are no longer in these situations, but you'd still like to understand why you made certain decisions. This exercise is great for bringing clarity to your past decision-making as well.

Questions to help guide you to clarity
Relationship Issues:
- I want you to go back in time to when you chose your partner. Look around your life. Were you happy with your financial life, your body/weight, your career, your social life, etc? Feel free to add other areas to question yourself. Only you know what was going on in your life that could have played a role in any decision-making. If you had improved those areas *before* you met them, would you still have chosen this person? Good to know, right? This will help guide you to fix these areas, and then you can decide if you want to stay with your current partner or reassess things. This exercise also works for any previous partners as well to help you understand why you chose them.

Career Issues:
- Let's say you are in a job where you are not satisfied. Instead of saying "I hate my job," allow yourself to look under the hood. You might ask yourself: What exactly is it about this job that I dislike the most? Is it my co-workers, lack of good pay, low energy, or no room for growth? Narrow it down to what bothers you the most. How can you fix it? If you hate the pay, can you go back to school or take classes to acquire a better skillset? Can you leverage your current experience to start your own business? Can you freshen up your resume and apply to higher paying positions? No more complaining allowed. Figure out what the exact problem is and get to work on fixing it.

Personal Issues:
- And lastly, let's say you are not happy, or you are depressed, but you can't quite figure out why. You could use these set of questions to help guide you to clarity: mentally go back to a time when you were in a happier state. What was different in your life back when you were happier? Were you exercising more often? Were you eating better? Were you hanging around more happy and positive people back then? Now, fast forward to your current life and ask the same questions. Am I still making exercise a priority? What is the quality of my friendships? In other words, there had to be a point in your life when you were once happy, right? So, mentally go back there and look around. What exactly was different in your internal and external world compared to today?

These are really important exercises that you don't want to skim over. Take your time answering these. Go deep. Go deeper if you can. Ask yourself specific questions around each situation, experience, person, job, etc. Get creative. Don't just rely on my categories. I want you to get under the hood of your life and try to pinpoint exactly what is making you unhappy.

Once you have the right answers to your questions, you can use them as leverage to help you make the necessary changes. You will slowly start to feel more empowered. How do I know? Because this is how our brain works. It systematically wants to solve any problem you have. It will help you if you engage with it. The more you practice this process, you will start the process of healing and creating change in your life. You will also develop the necessary mental and emotional tools that can help bring you closer to your goals, which means you will ultimately become a happier and more fulfilled person.

Chapter Five

Self-Love Mastery

Let's talk

I didn't understand the critical importance of practicing self-love until I was in my 40s. How sad is that? I liked myself fine and took good care of myself throughout the years, but I never made myself and my needs a priority as if I was my own caregiver. There's a big difference between simply doing acts to care for your needs and being intentional about your wellbeing, whether it be mentally, spiritually, physically, or emotionally. To me, that difference is defined by the mindset that precedes it.

The first part of my life would be best summed up as survival mode, followed by the chapter of becoming a mother and wife. It wasn't until my kids were grown and I entered a new chapter of life that I turned my energy inward and started giving myself the love and energy that I had been giving everyone else for years.

Lessons learned

When it comes to the topic of self-love, there's so many books, blogs, podcasts, and various other information sources floating around discussing this trendy topic and how to make it better. The problem is that most of these discuss only the surface level type of loving yourself and the things that you can do to improve it. I believe there is a deeper level of self-love that would require us to peel back the layers of how we truly see ourselves.

To be clear, the surface level ways of improving self-love are very important and should not be minimized. They are simply the appetizer and not the main course. Here are some of my favorite "surface level" ways to care for yourself and practice self-love:

- Keeping small promises to yourself each day, no matter how trivial, when you make a promise to yourself, keep it. This reinforces the idea that you matter!
- Saying NO to anything or anyone that steals your peace.
- Letting go of anything that you don't have control over.
- Creating a powerful morning routine.
- Making prayer or meditation a part of your daily habits. This reconnects you to the divine part of your spirit, the essence of who you are. It's mentally grounding and spiritually uplifting.
- Doing some form of exercise each day. This honors your physical body and creates the mindset that you are worthy of feeling great.
- Journaling - This is the most powerful way to get to know yourself. You can start with 3 simple journal prompts each day.

    1. **Today, I will:** *Fill in the blank of what your highest ideal or goal would be for that day. Example: Today, I will be more mindful. Today, I will complete Chapter 3 of my book.*
    2. **What reminder do I want to give myself today?** *Ex: I love that I will stay focused on my goals today. I appreciate this quality within myself.*
    3. **What's one thing I can do today to set myself up for success?** *Ex: I will time block by turning my*

phone off for 1 hour so I can concentrate on tackling my To Do list.

Self esteem vs self-image
Self-Esteem

I think we all agree that the higher our self-esteem, the less likely we will put up with negatvitiy in life or allow someone to mistreat us. But why is this true? It's because self-esteem is the engine that drives your perception of yourself. Think of a really expensive piece of jewelry. If you owned a rare diamond necklace, you wouldn't put it in the hands of someone who didn't value or care for it properly, right?

Like that valuable jewelry, if you perceive yourself as being of a high value, it would be a byproduct of higher self-esteem, hence the higher regard you have for yourself.

If you have an unhealthy opinion of yourself, there is always a reason why. The danger of having low self-esteem is that it affects every decision you make in your life. How you allow yourself to be treated by your friends and others is directly related to how much you like yourself.

Self-esteem and self-image are often thought of as the same thing, but they're not. These two are uniquely different, and yet they are also intertwined. Make no mistake, they both play a huge role in how much you love yourself and your level of happiness. Here is a simple way to understand the difference between the two. Your self-esteem is defined by how much you like yourself. And how much you like yourself is determined by your self-image.

Self-Image

What exactly is your self-image? Your self-image is the way you think of yourself and see yourself in your day-to-day interactions with others. In short, your self-image is how much you value yourself. Your self-image is shaped by the perception you have of yourself, also known as your self-ideal. Now get this: your self-ideal is made up of your values, goals, dreams, and aspirations.

Think of it like this: your self-esteem is how much you like yourself. Your self-image is how much you value yourself. While self-esteem and self-image are internal and part of who we think we are, the self-ideal is external, and it is a standard we set for ourselves to determine who we are capable of becoming.

Let's make this simple:

Your self-esteem = your self-image + your self-ideal. If you have low self-esteem, it can be traced right down to your self-ideal which is where your goals, virtues, dreams, and aspirations are found deep within you. Simply put, if you don't have proper goals, if your values are not clear, if you don't have clear aspirations and dreams, then guess what? Your self-ideal is broken. And the problem with a broken self-ideal is that it is the gas that drives the vehicle of your self-image. And guess what suffers when your self-image is distorted or blurry? Your self-esteem takes this hit, over and over in your life, until you fix the underlying issues.

Psychologists have discovered that the more your behavior is consistent with what you feel your ideal self should be, the more you tend to like and respect yourself.

What does all this mean for you? When you are working towards your goals and the things that make you feel better about who you are as a person, you feel more in love with yourself. You feel happier because you are being consistent with your highest ideals. On the other hand, when you behave in a way that is inconsistent with your highest ideals, you experience a negative self-image. When you feel yourself performing below your best, below what you truly aspire to do, your self-esteem and levels of happiness decrease.

> *Sometimes we have to have grace and patience with ourselves as we rebuild our self-esteem and self-image. Try this: Say to yourself every day, "I love myself as I was, as I am, and as I am becoming". This is a quick, but powerful affirmation!*
>
> ~ Diamond Leone

How self-love plays out in our relationships

I believe the reason why some people tolerate unhealthy relationships and friendships is because they don't have a healthy ideal of themselves. They haven't taken the time to figure out what they truly want out of life. Maybe they were never taught how to do this or maybe they simply don't feel a better way is even possible for them. I am here to tell you that you can absolutely fix this area of your life. But just like anything else, you must be intentional about it. You must know you deserve better.

Once you sit down and write out your goals, make a list of actionable items that you need to do to complete those goals, and assign strict deadlines, something magical happens. Your self-ideal becomes more defined and empowered which then increases your self-esteem. Your self-love also increases, making it less likely that you will allow someone to mistreat you. You will grow out of the unhealthy way of thinking and living that you may be used to. You shift the focus off of what's wrong in your life and you begin to focus on YOURSELF! This is the act of working on your "self-ideal". (Remember earlier how I explained that your self-ideal consists of your goals, values, etc.? This is it, baby! This is how you fix a broken self-ideal). This is what popular wisdom is now referring to as "inner work." You are now doing the necessary work to pull yourself together and fix these broken areas deep inside your heart and mind.

Your self-esteem will start to rise, but more importantly, your vibrational level will increase. You will naturally start to love yourself more because you are respecting and caring for yourself. Here's an analogy: Remember how you felt when you got your first new car? Even if it was used, it was still new to you. You took such great care of it. You washed it, waxed it, made sure it had air fresheners or new floor mats. If someone rode in your car, you would never let them leave trash in it or put their feet up on the dash. You would certainly never let anyone smoke in your car, and even if you smoked, you still most likely wouldn't even smoke in your own car. Why is this? Because you cared about your vehicle. It was special to you. That feeling of pride every time you walked towards your car made you feel good about yourself. You'd invested your hard-earned money on something that was worthwhile to you. Think of yourself like this car. You are now taking better care of yourself. You are investing in yourself, your greatest asset and you will be less likely to let anyone mistreat you ever again.

How it all works together

Remember, how we said earlier that like attracts like? This is how vibrational energy works. You will progressively pursue something that is important to YOU, and therefore, you'll attract people and circumstances on this new higher vibrational frequency. The toxic behaviors that you put up with in your past will not be tolerated. You will naturally gravitate towards the positive people and things that align with this new way of loving yourself. You will have taken back all your power in your own life. This is an AMAZING FEELING!

Chapter Six
Defining Your Core Values

Let's talk

If you baked a delicious chocolate cake and offered me a slice and I loved it, I might ask you for the recipe. Let's say you gave it to me, and I took the list of ingredients to the grocery store so that I could buy them with the intention of coming back home and baking this yummy cake for myself. However, once I arrive at the store, I suddenly realize that I am short on time and so I decide to go rogue and buy some random ingredients because I don't feel like looking at the list and being disciplined or patient enough to go through the aisles of the store and get the specific ingredients required by the recipe. When I arrive back home, I try to make this cake and follow the recipe you gave me, but since I don't have the exact ingredients, I do the best I can with what I have. My cake turns out disgusting, and I am so angry and confused as to how this could have happened. I call you the next day to complain about it.

What would you tell me? I think you would first laugh at my mistakes; I mean let's be honest, how could you not? This is what happens when we try to live a life that is not in alignment with our core values.

Lessons learned

Before we dive deeper, let me explain why I added this chapter on core values. In the last chapter on self-love mastery, we talked about how your self-ideal is made up of your goals, virtues, aspirations and of course your values. I want you to understand how to clarify what your true values are and why they are important. You'd be surprised how many people do not know these. Principle #2 is about helping you to expand your awareness of self. Inside each one of us is a driving force called our value system and the psychological factors that make us tick. These are the equivalent to the list of ingredients in our analogy about baking a cake. When we understand how this internal system is designed and how it plays a huge role in our happiness, we begin to think differently about the choices that we make in our daily lives. Things start to come full circle with respect to our happiness or lack thereof.

What are values?

Your values are a set of beliefs for which you have an emotional investment, either for or against something, and hold true for yourself and your life. It's what you stand for. Your values are what make you the person you are. Your chief responsibility in life should be to clarify your values. It's important to note that values are not something we "select". Rather they are discovered and revealed through observing your behaviors and decisions. Knowing exactly what you believe in and stand for will be the barometer upon which all your decisions are based. If you're confused about the difference between self-esteem and core values, think of it like this: Self-esteem gives you the courage to execute the right decisions for yourself but knowing your core values are the information upon which you base your decisions. It's why you choose one thing over another. When you are living in complete alignment with what you believe to be right and true, you will feel happy and positive about yourself and your world.

The reverse is also true. When you have feelings of unhappiness and stress about a circumstance or situation in your life, it is probably because you have made choices in your life that contradicted your values. Please, read that sentence again. When you are highly stressed about certain events, people, relationships, a job, or projects, there is likely something within those situations not in alignment with your inner values.

Past experiences discover our values

Maybe you're not sure what your values are. The easiest and simplest way to tell what your values are is to examine your past behavior. Your true values are always demonstrated in your actions under pressure. When you must make one decision over the other and your back is against the wall, you are going to choose the option that is consistent with what is most valuable and important to you. So, think back to a time when you had to make a really important decision under pressure. The choice that you ultimately decided to go with is a clear indicator of where your values were at that time.

Here are some other questions to help you discover your values:

- How do I want to feel in life and why?
- Which people inspire me and why?
- What do I always talk about doing but never get around to doing?

- If I could make one radical change in my life right now, what would it be and why?
- What's missing from my life and why?
- In the past, what choices did I make with my free time or excess money?
- What makes me feel important?
- What raises my self-esteem?
- What have I accomplished in the past that has given me my greatest sense of reward or accomplishment?
- What increases my sense of self-respect or pride?

Answering the above questions will help you to understand why you have chosen one choice over another. Look for patterns in your answers. Do you see a need for security? A need to feel significant? To help others? A need to feel loved? This exercise is important because your answers will help you to see your decisions differently.

> *"It's not hard to make decisions when you know what your values are."*
> ~ Roy Disney

Your values in the 5 areas of your life

As mentioned earlier, you are the happiest when you are doing on the outside what is congruent with your values on the inside. There are five key areas of your life. Whether you realize it or not, you currently have values for each of these areas. Virtually, all of your life scenarios will fit into these following five categories:

1. Your health/personal growth
2. Your finances
3. Your career
4. Your family/relationships

5. Your spiritual connection/contribution to others

Let's examine each one of these closely and see if you can answer the questions for each area. If you're willing to put in the time to answer these questions, I believe you will come out of this chapter with a clearer idea of what your core values are. As you read the questions out loud, pay attention to how you feel. Write down the answers that resonate the most with you in each category. You will find that you have some core values in all of these categories, but there will be one that sticks out more than the others as you read them. Look at your life as it is and compare it to the areas below. Ask yourself which of these areas do you tend to spend the most time?

Your health/personal growth

What are your values today about your *health and personal growth*? Do you believe in the values of self-mastery, self-control, and self-discipline? Do you set goals and place a high priority on a healthy lifestyle and make whatever sacrifices necessary to stay on track to achieve them? When health and personal growth are important to you, you spend time each day devoted to exercise, reading and learning, eating healthier and your mind and body reflect that. You hold yourself to higher standards in these areas of your life. Structure and things like having a morning routine are important to you.

Your finances/career

What are your values about your *money and career*? Do you believe in the values of hard work, education, quality work, investing, entrepreneurship? If these areas are most important to you, you tend to naturally have money saved, you look for ways to climb the corporate ladder or you are tenacious about starting your own business. Having a financial nest egg or a solid plan to retire early is of extreme importance to you.

Your family/relationships

What are your values regarding your *family and personal relationships*? When this area of your life is most significant to you, you will turn down financial opportunities if it interferes with quality time with your partner or family. You believe in the importance of honesty, compassion, consistency, emotional security, and unconditional love. When you practice these values consistently, you tend to have more rewarding relationships and people tend to easily feel connected to you.

Your spiritual connection/contribution to others

What are your values regarding *spirituality and giving back to others?* Do you believe in the values of serving, honoring, generosity, strengthening, and supporting others? When you live your life according to these values, you have a sense of belonging and a deeper sense of purpose in life. You take the suffering of others to heart and take action to help without hesitation. When this value is most important to you, your time and resources are allocated to reflect the heart of someone who feels more connected to their source energy when they are in the spirit of serving and giving.

Once you have identified your values for each of these areas, you should try to live your life congruent with them. The way you do that is by devoting more of your time and life in these areas. Stay as close to them as you can. This is key to being truly fulfilled and happy.

Re-examining your values over time

You may be thinking, "But isn't it possible that my values can change over time?" Absolutely they can, which is why you want to re-examine them periodically.

Socrates once said, "The unexamined life is not worth living". As the seasons of your life change, so might some of your values. You will have to stop yourself from time to time to reexamine them. Afterall, this is the equivalent of your "ingredients list" when you are going through the aisles of the store shopping or in this case, strolling through the aisles of life making major decisions. You will have to ask yourself "what are my values in this area of my life right now?" You may find that your values change as you get older, and this is perfectly normal. As your priorities change over time, you will have to adjust and modify your values accordingly to reflect what you believe.

Since the whole purpose of this book is to learn how to get your happy back, remember this: The happiest people in the world today are those who have taken the time to identify what their values are and work hard every day to make choices that align with those values. Whenever you are experiencing stress of any kind, stop and ask yourself, "In what way am I compromising my innermost values in this situation?"

There are no guarantees that life will go as planned, but at least if you take the time to identify your values and know what you stand for, you have a fighting chance to select the right people and circumstances for your life. And more importantly, you will know when to say no to things that don't line up with the person you are or the life you want to have. How cool is that?

Principle #3
Create Your Mental Tool Kit

In this principle, we will be discussing how to become a mental samurai

- Determine your true goals

- Mindset matters

- Using the power of visualization

LET'S GET STARTED!

Chapter Seven
Determine Your True Goals

Let's talk

In Principle #1, I shared a little bit of my story to help you understand that my early life was anything but fun. It was filled with so much uncertainty, stress, poverty, and sadness. That's the hand that I was dealt, and maybe you were dealt a similar hand in your early life. Maybe your hardships came later as you were in your teenage years, or maybe you're going through them right now. We all have a cross to bear in life. None of us make it through without being challenged to grow in some way or another.

As I mentioned previously, I wouldn't change a thing about my past. I have learned so many valuable lessons as a result of those hard times, but more importantly, I have learned to overcome hardships and create happiness within each day as I go along, and you can, too! One of the things that really helped me to do this was to always, always, always have a goal that I am working towards. Always! They say the moment you put a deadline on a dream, it becomes a goal. Let's talk a little bit about what goals are and how they work on a macro and micro level.

Lessons learned

When it comes to success and setting goals, the most important word to remember is "clarity." There is a direct relationship between the level of clarity you have about who you are, what you want, and virtually everything you accomplish in life. H.L. Hunt was a former bankrupt cotton farmer who went on to become a multi-billionaire before his death in 1974. He was once asked during an interview what advice he could give to others who were trying to become financially successful. He said there are only two things required: First, you must decide exactly what it is you want to accomplish. Most people never do that in their entire lives. And secondly, you must determine what price you'll have to pay, and then resolve to pay that price.

Goal seeking is an automatic function

We've already covered that you absolutely can control your own thoughts. But did you know that since your thoughts are what control your actions and your mood, you have the ability, through your thoughts, to bring into existence the very things that you think about on a consistent basis. Brian Tracy, a world-renowned business expert and highly sought-after speaker says, "You become what you think about most of the time." It's like your thoughts are a precursor and have the power to guide your reality.

Do you pay attention to what you are thinking about most of the time? It's a learned skill that you can use to your advantage. Now, imagine if you set clear, measured, and time specific goals around these things that you think about. For example, do you have thoughts about making more money? Having a better career? Buying a home? Getting out of debt? Losing weight? Whatever it is, you can set a clear goal.

When you set a goal, write it down, and give it a deadline. You will activate a part of your subconscious brain that tells your conscious mind to direct all your faculties and powers to achieve it. This is how it works: you have an automatic goal-seeking mechanism located deep within your brain. It has generative and sustaining power that will push you and motivate you subconsciously. This is accomplished through repetitious thought because your mind pays attention to what you think about most of the time. It's like your own little universe knows that this is on your agenda, and it must be done. When you are clear about your goal, you do not need to know where your goal is or how to achieve it. By simply deciding what you want, you will start moving unerringly towards your goals, and your goals will suddenly start to move unerringly toward you. It really is quite amazing!

> *"If you limit your goals to what you know you can achieve, you are setting the bar way too low."*
> ~ Ray Dalio (Billionaire and Hedge Fund manager)

What happens if you don't set goals?

If we have the ability to set clear, measurable, and time specific goals and are born with the automatic, goal-seeking mechanism, then why do so few people have goals? There are four reasons why people fail to set goals.

1. They think goals are not important

The first reason that I believe people don't have goals is because they don't realize the importance of setting goals. When I was growing up and all through college, the topic of having or setting goals was never discussed. It was never taught in any of the schools. Learning how to set goals is one of the most important skills you could ever know. Everything in your life should be based on goals. If you want to earn more money, you should set a goal. If you want to travel the world, set a goal. If you want to have a better marriage, set a goal. Goals are the engine in the car that drives your happiness!

2. They don't know how

Secondly, most people think they already have goals when what they really have is a "want" list. Examples of this are: "I want to make more money," "I want to lose weight," "I want to buy a house," or "I want to start my own business one day." These are NOT goals but wants.

A goal is distinctively different because it must be SMART. This acronym stands for:

S-specific
M-measurable
A-attainable
R-realistic
T-time specific.

Using one of the examples above, you could say, "I want to lose 30 pounds within a six-month period." This is a very specific, measurable, attainable, realistic and time-based goal. Do you see the difference between a wish versus an actual goal? Do you feel the power of how the latter is more achievable because it is specific, measurable, and has a deadline attached? This is the power of knowing how to properly set goals.

3. They have a fear of failure

The third reason that people don't set goals is because they are afraid that they will fail.

Failure is very scary and intimidating for everyone. Nothing is more devastating to your self-esteem than to wake up one day and realize that you are not where you want to be in life. This happens to a lot of people. It has happened to me, too. We lose so much time focusing on the mundane chores and tasks of everyday life that we forget to chart our course. We forget to plan where we are going. I am here to tell you that you must set goals, no matter how small they might seem at first. Depending on the current challenges in your life, I can understand why you might put off setting goals. For example, if you are struggling with your health goals as most of us do, you may not be so quick to set goals in this area for fear of not meeting those goals and feeling like a failure. I get it. However, not setting goals will guarantee failure. You can't hit a target that you can't see. As my Beyonce alter ego would say, "Get over yourself!" Set your goals, and if you fail, who cares? Dust yourself off, and try again. At least you know what you are aiming for.

4. They have a fear of rejection from their peers

The fourth reason people fail to set goals is the fear of rejection. They are afraid that if they set a goal and don't achieve it, others will criticize or ridicule them. When I set out to write this book, I had so much self-doubt. Who would read it? Would it be good enough? Was I even qualified enough to be writing a book? Would people make fun of my thoughts and ideas? You know what? *Stop that nonsense!* These are misleading self-limiting beliefs at play. This is our fragile ego trying to protect us from failure. It's what the brain does. The bigger your dream, the bigger the resistance you will face. Always remember that! No one has it all figured out. The key is to set goals and *get started!*

You must push through and set a small goal each day toward your project and go for it! The results will come, and you will feel so excited as you do this! You will be building momentum with each smaller goal you accomplish. And before you know it, you won't care what anyone else has to say. You will be proving to yourself that you are *more* than capable, *more* than smart enough! You will be creating your fearlessness as you go! That's how amazing you are!

Chapter Eight

Mindset Matters

Let's talk

If you remember one thing from this entire book, please remember this: The mind is a battlefield! Most battles we fight are either won or lost in the mind first. I don't know about you, but I believe as as we get older, our mind just seems to get heavier. Maybe it's because we are carrying around years of hurt feelings and baggage. Years of triumphs and failures. Some days will be better than others. Getting control of your mind can be hard work, but it's the difference between being happy and, well, unhappy.

You must learn to control negative thoughts, or they can grow bigger over time. I hated my father for years. I was angry at myself for longing for him, even though I knew he was incapable of giving me the love I deserved. Years went on, and I felt like I was doing okay with it all. Then my marriage ended. Here comes another emotional struggle where I had to break open parts of myself all over again to learn, to forgive and to grow. Maybe you might see some of yourself in my story. I hate to be the bearer of bad news, but this is life. Maybe it's a business you started that didn't turn out so well. You had a new business idea and that went bust as well. These are all a part of our journey here on this planet. Sometimes, you will want to blame others, but the truth is you are the common denominator in every scenario. So, it's going be up to you friend, to learn how to navigate them in a way that serves you.

I want to take a moment to differentiate between the practice of being mindful versus an empowered mindset. Being mindful refers to the being aware of and fully present to your thoughts, feelings, environment, and body sensations. We observe these without judgement of right and wrong or time and place. Practicing mindfulness is also associated with meditation. This is an important transformational practice that is part of getting your happy back, and you will want to make this part of your routine self-care. However, this chapter focuses on creating an empowered mindset, which is the support structure on which we will build a powerful platform for all other life strategies.

Lessons learned

It took me years to understand the concept of a healthy mindset and how we can use it to create unlimited happiness and an empowered mental state. The definition of mindset is "a set of beliefs or a way of thinking that determines one's behavior, outlook and mental attitude." There are two types of mindsets: a fixed mindset and a growth mindset. When you have a fixed mindset, you believe that these qualities are inborn, fixed, and unchangeable. When you have a growth mindset, you believe these qualities can be developed and strengthened with time and experience.

You get to decide which type of mindset you will have. Regardless of what anyone tells you, you do have the ability to control your future through fostering a growth mindset and actively learning ways to expand your skillset and way of thinking. People with a growth mindset show a greater ability to handle life's challenges. They have more resilience and are more likely to have success and happiness in their life.

Our mindset shapes the world that we live in and creates our reality. If you have found that you are not experiencing the happiness that you know you deserve, then you have to change the way you are thinking. Your mindset needs to be reprogrammed! To reprogram our mind, we must first create a set of intentional behaviors that can help us control the dialogue that occurs inside our head.

But first, understand this basic concept: *You cannot stop thinking negative thoughts.*

The mind does not work that way. For example, if I said "Do NOT think about red apples." The first thing you would see in your mind is red apples. The only way to get rid of negative thoughts is to replace them with new, more positive thoughts. This was the game changer for me.

When you purposely make the decision that you want more happiness and a better life, the universe opens up, and it aligns itself to your new decisions. This is the law of inspired action working for you. When you discipline yourself and decide that you are going to take action by setting goals, your mindset shifts. You start harnessing your true power. We talked earlier about how our thoughts have energy. The Law of Attraction states that whatever thoughts we hold in our mind, these very things will manifest back to us in some way. Therefore, it's critical to redirect and stomp out any negative thoughts as soon as they creep up.

> *"Our greatest battles are that with our minds"*
> ~ *Jameson Fran*

Building a positive mindset and strengthening it through conditioning and following this new intentional set of behaviors really works. I tend to be a very analytical thinker, so I appreciate when an author describes a strategy and practical application of techniques. That said, if you are really enjoying this content so far and want to go deeper, then, do I have a treat for you!

Empowered mindset techniques you can try

If you want a major shift in your way of thinking, I have put together three techniques that you can implement over the next seven days to help you get started in developing an empowered mindset and reprogram limiting beliefs.

Now, let's have some fun! I want you to incorporate these techniques into your daily life:

TECHNIQUE # 1 - Create a positive affirmation and say it out loud to yourself every day, while using the "Incantation Method."

> You've all heard of affirmations, which is a set of positive phrases that you repeat to yourself until your mind rewires itself to believe them and act. However, we are going to take these to the next level using incantation, which uses your physiology while you are saying the affirmations. Incantations are about embodying the meaning behind the words while also using the movement of your body to emotionally charge your brain. Combining these will reprogram your mind much faster.
>
> Write out your affirmations first. Get out a piece of paper and think of the area of your life that needs to be changed the most. You want to write your affirmation as

a proclamation of what is already taking place right now! Make sure it has the following components:

- Must be in first person, use present tense
- State it in a positive context
- Be specific as possible
- Use action wording ending in "ing"

Below is a fun example:

"I am smart, **hot** as hell, and everyone wants to be around me. I am funny, outgoing, and I have so much positive energy flowing through me," OR "I am a successful business owner making (Fill in your $ amount here) a year, I have an amazingly supportive partner, and I am driving the new Tesla (fill in current model). My life feels AMAZING!"

Next, let's create the incantation while using your body. Keep it simple until you memorize this. I would find a place where you can take a walk on an even pathway so you can read your affirmation while you are walking without tripping or falling. Or maybe a stationary exercise bike where you can't fall off while you're reading. Some people can read while on a tread mill, but I personally cannot. The point is you want your body moving. Get creative here.

Another good idea is to record your affirmation into the voice memo on your phone. Leave enough of a pause after each recorded sentence so you can repeat the affirmation out loud after hearing it. This way, you can be running, riding a bicycle, etc., while you play your voice memo. As you hear your original recorded affirmation, repeat the affirmation back aloud. The goal is to say these affirmations while you are moving your body. The concept here is that energy flows where attention goes. When you put physiology, energy and the power of intention behind your positive words, you are taking manifestation to a whole different level, while also incorporating the power of visualization. It's like the ultimate mind-changing cocktail.

It may sound hard to believe, but trust me, you are reprogramming the messages you create in your brain. There are numerous studies on the power of using daily affirmations. But now adding the power of incantations, you will become unstoppable. Even if you think it's silly, just do it for one week and watch your life start to change!

Here's another example of a positive affirmation I have used in my life. Perhaps it can help guide you to create your own:

I am AMAZED at the abundant life that I am living! I have so much love within me to share with others, and I am finding new ways to express this love in a healthy way each day. I love to experience joy, and I am delighted to be making it a priority to receive this happiness into my life. I look for ways to see the positivity in everything that happens to me. My optimism is a true gift from God, and I am so thankful for it. I abound in creativity and entrepreneurship, and I look for every opportunity to use these gifts to enrich my life and to help others. I am wealthy in ways I have yet to discover. I am excited to watch my bank account increase because I can use these blessings to enrich the lives of others. I am so thankful for the time I have been gifted on this planet to serve others. I am using all my positivity, personal growth, and self-love within me to attract the right life partner. I am capable of more than I could ever imagine. I am devoted to growing, learning, forgiving, loving, sharing, and manifesting in all that I say and do.

Do you see how I am saying things as if they are already taking place in my life? When you read my sample affirmation, pay attention to how you feel. You may notice that you start to feel optimistic and hopeful. Affirmations are incredibly powerful. If you need help writing an affirmation specific to an area of your life, you can do some research online; there are plenty of free resources to help guide you.

TECHNIQUE #2 - For every negative thing that you say to yourself or is said to you, turn it into an empowering question.

Example: "I look fat in this dress" can be changed to "how can I look slimmer in my clothes?"
This puts you in a solution-seeking mode which means you come out of any possible "victim mindset" and your brain will seek out an answer that can instantly change your whole paradigm. Asking empowered questions will give you empowered answers! Remember, this is a powerful tool to create the right mindset. Keep asking yourself these types of questions especially when you feel frustrated or things are not going your way. One of my favorite empowering questions is "why is this happening for me instead of asking "why is this happening to me." Notice the shift of feeling empowered versus powerless.

TECHNIQUE #3 - Learn how to motivate yourself.

I know sometimes it may seem that you are at the mercy of how you feel on any given day. For example, on a good day, you may feel that you will do well, and on a bad day you might feel that you are unmotivated, procrastinate, and achieve very little. Well, let me tell you, you don't have to be at the mercy of how you feel! Know this friend, that you are not your feelings. Feelings do not equal reality. You must accept that your emotions and your mood are yours to control. Remember that motion changes emotion. Either change your physical state or change your reward to something bigger that gets you excited. You can recharge yourself by going for a 15-minute walk, doing some jumping jacks, or getting your heart rate up. After that, try working on your To-Do List again. Lastly, never underestimate the power of a good reward.

For every task that you may not be excited to do, try this: reward yourself with something enjoyable or fun after you accomplish it. It could be something simple like going for ice cream, lighting candles, or taking a hot bath. Maybe going for a massage or phoning a friend. Or even buying yourself a new outfit. That's my favorite one. Regardless of the exact reward, make it something you'll really enjoy. So many people overlook this small detail, but it really works to get you motivated.

Chapter Nine
Using The Power Of Visualization

Let's talk

When I was a young girl, I remember my mom giving me the "college talk." My college talk was probably a little unconventional and unlike what most kids would get.

"College is stupid and a waste of time," my mom would say. "If you want to make real money in life, start your own business and invest in real estate." I would argue back, asking that if college was so dumb, then why do so many people do it? Mom was unrelenting, "Because people do what they're told. They don't think for themselves. They don't know what their ultimate goals are in life, and they think going to college will make them successful. It will not. The only thing college does is it grooms you to work for someone else."

I would argue back that I was going to go to college, and I didn't care what she said. That's how I said it in my head anyway. I darn sure didn't say it like that to her. I think I may have mentioned earlier that I was terrified of my mom for good reason. She was not to be played with. She said, "Go ahead and waste years of your life going to a school to learn about crap that will never make you a dime, only to owe a huge school loan that will take you years to pay back.

You'll come back one day asking me to show you how to make real money, 'cause they don't teach that in college".

You can imagine how angry I was listening to my mother putting down college. Especially when we were barely able to put food on the table and had suffered periods of homelessness. How dare she! For me, going to college represented a better way of life. It's what smart people did. People who had homes to live in and food to put inside their refrigerators all went to college. College is what I wanted. She made it seem like I was aspiring to join a traveling circus as a stagehand. Most parents would love to have a child that was eager to attend school. What was wrong with her?

Why am I talking about all of this? Going to college was something more than just a thought for me. It was my plan and something that I wanted to do with all my heart. I had already visualized myself graduating so many times. I had visions of myself walking across a huge stage in my cap and gown, smiling and waving to my friends and family. Anyway, this was my fantasy, my wish, my dream, and I wanted it. I kept this visual in my head often. When I had to drop out of high school to get a job, I was disappointed and felt discouraged. Not because I had to get a job; I was excited to work and make money. It was because I felt I was moving farther away from my dream of attending college. You see, you must have a high school degree or equivalent to get into college, and quitting high school was not part of my master plan. This is a prime example of how life can throw you curve balls. Even though I never made it through high school, I never quit visualizing walking across that stage.

After working a few years, I signed up for a GED (General Education Degree) program. I went on to attend college and graduated with a 4-year degree in only two and half years with honors. And yes, I did walk across that stage in my cap and gown! I can't explain the feeling you have when you visualize something happening in your life and then it comes true. It's almost like you're dreaming, but you're not, you're living it! You are living out what your mind has been seeing all along. This is the power of visualization! It really does work!

By the way, my mom was right about college debt and how it can cripple young adults financially. I was too young to understand what she was trying to explain to me. I ended up working a full-time job during the day while also attending college full-time at night and paying for all my classes along the way. I graduated with no student loans thanks to my mom's lectures about debt. I learned to be strategic and find jobs that had great tuition reimbursement programs. Thanks, Mom!

> "You are more productive by doing fifteen minutes of visualization than from sixteen hours of hard labor."
> ~Abraham Hicks

Lessons learned

We've talked about the importance of having the right mindset and setting goals. Here in Principle 3, you are learning to create a powerful mental toolkit using the power of mindset and now visualization. Let's try and understand how visualization can be used as a powerful tool to help you achieve your goals.

What is visualization?

Visualization is the ability to hold a thought or an image in your mind for an extended period. By doing this, you activate your subconscious to work on bringing these thoughts into reality. This *conscious creation* is one of the most powerful faculties we have as human beings. No other creatures have this amazing power! How cool is that? Many people are unaware of these superpowers and fail to use them for goal attainment. That is exactly what it is designed for! It's not enough to just say what you want, although there is power in that, too, but you must visualize it as if it has already happened.

How does visualization work?

Visualization activates the law of attraction which draws into your life the people, circumstances, and resources that you need to achieve your goals. All improvement in your life begins with an improvement in your mentality. You are what you are and where you are today largely because of the mental pictures you are holding currently in your conscious mind. As you change your mental picture on the inside, your outside world will begin to change to correspond with those pictures.

In Rhonda Byrne's bestselling book *The Secret*, she explains how each one of us has the innate ability to change the direction of our lives simply by focusing intently on our thoughts. These thoughts, whether positive or negative, program our subconscious mind and initiate the law of attraction that pushes us towards the direction of our dominant thoughts. When you begin to tap into the power of your subconscious mind, you are tapping into another whole dimension of power. You will start to achieve more in a year or two than most people achieve in a lifetime. You will begin to move more rapidly towards your goals than you can imagine!

There are four parts of visualization:

- **Frequency** - The more times you repeat a clear mental picture of exactly what you want, the more rapidly your subconscious mind will commit it to memory and go to work to make this a reality.

- **Duration** - Hold this mental image of what you want in your mind. The longer you can hold your mental picture, the more rapidly it will be impressed into your subconscious mind and the faster it will manifest into your life.
- **Vividness** - This is how clearly you see your goal or desired outcome. The more you write it down, review it, and repeat it mentally, the clearer it will become. Then it will appear in your world exactly as you imagined it.
- **Intensity** - This is the amount of emotion and feeling that you associate with your mental image. You must allow yourself to feel it as if it has already been given to you. How do you feel now that you have it? This is perhaps one of the most important aspects of visualization. Once you have a clear mental image of what your goal is and you practice the element of intensely focusing on it, the universe knows you are serious. The Law of Attraction is then engaged, and you and your goals start moving unerringly toward each other at a rapid pace.

Beware of negative visualization

The power of visualization is neutral. This means that like a two-edged knife, it can cut in both directions. Visualization brings you whatever you intensely focus on whether good or be bad, so be very careful to only focus on the desired outcome. Did you know that if you tend to worry a lot, you are still practicing a form of visualization? Many people don't realize this.

Since worry is a form of negative goal-setting, you are engaging in the process of thinking about, imagining and visualizing the exact thing you DO NOT want to happen. Don't let this scare you but do let it guide you on what NOT to do. Remember, only focus on the positive outcomes and the positive goals you desire! You can do it!

Chapter Ten
The Art Of Reframing Your Story

Let's talk

Look, I know I've talked quite a bit about my childhood in this book. I promise I have other stories and lessons to share as I grew. That said, there were some amazing life lessons learned in my childhood, and I want to take you to the scene of the crime where one of these lessons originated. Some were embarrassing and funny, and others, of course, were sad. But the thing I'm most proud of is the perspective on life these lessons taught me and the person I've become as a result.

During my stint in the 8th grade, and yes, I'm referring to this as one would a prison term, I felt extremely insecure about myself. I was tall, skinny, and couldn't seem to find any pants that looked right on my gangly frame. My butt was flat as a pancake. All the other girls were so pretty, curvy, and wore nice clothes. I felt like an alien from a galaxy far away. One last thing that I feel is important to mention. I developed my very first crush on a boy named Henry Salazar. My heart skipped a beat every time I saw his cute face in the school cafeteria. Henry may have smiled at me once or twice, I think. Or maybe he was smiling at a pretty girl behind me. It doesn't matter much. In my mind,

I was convinced Henry liked me. Henry, if you ever read this, know that my imaginary relationship with you was the highlight of most days back then.

Back to my story.

It was near the end of the school day, and I was waiting inside with the other kids to be picked up from school. Barreling down the carpool lane came the ugliest old beat-up van I'd ever seen. To make matters worse, plastered on the side of the van were huge words that read, "JESUS IS LORD!" All of the kids erupted in laughter. Heck, I started laughing at it, too. I mean, come on! Who on earth would come pick up their kid from school in such an eyesore? Next thing I knew, the van stopped and out popped my mom wearing a muumuu outfit. A muumuu! In case you don't know what that is, it's like wrapping a bedsheet around yourself and calling it a dress. And shallowly, I will explain that my mom was only 5 feet, 5 inches tall and very overweight, which made it look that much worse. All of the kids' heads turned toward me with the precision of Olympic synchronized swimmers and started pointing and laughing loudly. In case you were wondering, that is what it feels like when you want to die from embarrassment.

I ran to the nearest bathroom to collect myself. I stood inside the stall, wanting to cry from complete humiliation. This was not happening. Did Henry see any of this, I wondered. I wanted to die! It was bad enough to be poor and to look like a skinny alien, but now I had to be picked up by the Messiah's moving billboard? Then something rose inside of me. I knew this feeling all too well. It was the fighter inside me. You can knock me down as many times as you want, but she came back alive and picked me up as she does every single time. I don't know who she is at this point in my life, but I know she's in there. Because she has rescued me before.

I pulled myself together. I told myself I had two choices. I could continue to allow these kids to taunt me and make me feel like a loser and an outcast, or I could change the way I looked at this. What if I could laugh at this, too? On that day, I learned to change the narrative in my head. I told myself a different story than the limiting one those kids wanted me to believe.

I realized I could take the same humor they wanted to use as a sword to stab me and also use it as a shield. Where I come from, we call this flipping the script. I marched my skinny, flat-butt out of that bathroom, walked right past all the laughing hyenas, and said, "Laugh all you want. Now, if you'll excuse me, I've got a meeting with Jesus." I walked out of the school. I'm serious when I tell you something fierce grew inside me that day. I decided to no longer be ashamed. Enough with constantly being embarrassed. Enough with caring what other people think of me. It's too heavy.

As I climbed into the Jesus van, I gave my mom the stare of a runner who had just made it across the finish line of a race they didn't sign up for. I said we should probably get out of here. I admired my mom. She was never ever boring. Being raised by this woman was like being in a real-life sitcom. You never knew what was going to happen next. My mom was either fearless or just lived in her own bubble. Or maybe it was a bit of both. She was not put on this earth to impress others. I mean, clearly. Showing up to my school wearing a muumuu, without a care about what anyone else thought was a pretty gangster move. And quite honestly, it deserved a little respect. I told myself that no one else's mom would have the courage to do the things she did. Noticing my weird stare, she looked at me and asked with an oblivious smile, "So honey, how do you like the van?" "It's nice Mom, if you work for the Lord," I said.

> *"The rate at which a person can mature is directly proportionate to the amount of embarrassment they can tolerate"*
>
> ~ Douglas Engelbart

Lessons learned

Was I mortified when the event above was unfolding? Absolutely yes, I was. But at some point, you have to decide that you are fed up with being kicked around by life. That's what happened to me on that day. I refused to let someone else dictate the meaning of what something would be for me. You can't pick your parents, and you can't pick the set of circumstances you're born into. If you came from a family that did not have much money, you had to be tough. I got teased a lot. I got laughed at even more. But through it all, I learned to laugh at myself louder and faster than anyone else could. From that day forward, those kids could no longer get in my head because by the time they tried to laugh and make fun of me, I was already laughing at myself. I took their power away by using this strategy. I could find the humor in almost anything, which later became my superpower when life handed me difficult situations. This, along with many other experiences in life, taught me that a situation, circumstance, or event can only have the power that you give it. When you reframe any unpleasant story and give it an empowering meaning, you strip it of its power to hurt you.

What is reframing

You may be thinking, "Well, this story is entertaining, but what does it have to do with my life as an adult with real, grown-up world problems?" I didn't understand it at the time, but I had learned to use a technique called *reframing*. When something happens to you, your brain gives it a meaning based off previous experiences or belief systems. The meaning that it assigns to your situation is what is called a frame. It's how you present it to yourself. When those kids were laughing at me, my current frame was presenting a story that told me I should be ashamed. It told me that I was poor and should be embarrassed that I couldn't be picked up from school in a normal-looking vehicle because I wasn't worthy enough. Ouch, and no thanks! As a young kid, I chose humor as my new frame. I reframed my old story with a new frame, and I was able to see it as something funny instead of shameful. This powerful strategy can work for us now as adults, too and the beauty is that you can use any frame your heart desires.

Applying reframing to your life

The most effective tool for creating personal change is learning how to put the best frame on any experience. If you have been through an event in your life that you are not proud of such as divorce, bankruptcy, bad break up, betrayal of a friendship, etc., you can decide right now that you will reframe your story. You can choose a new story that either helps you to find the hidden lesson in that experience, or you can choose to find the dark humor in it so you can laugh at it, like I did in the story above. Or if you've experienced an unfortunate event such as the loss of a loved one, health issues, or something that you had no control over, you can reframe it with an empowering meaning that changes your perspective when you remember it.

After all, reframing is not about pretending that things are great when they are not. Rather, it's about discovering what could be great and choosing to present that version to yourself.

For example: You just lost your job.

Current frame: You feel devastated because your family is going to have to scale back on spending, and you won't be able to take the family vacation you had planned.

New frame: You'll look for another job but add the new skillsets you've learned over the past few years at your old job, which now make you more marketable and possibly qualify for a higher paying position somewhere else. Also, you are going to research ideas for your family to volunteer and give back to your local community while simultaneously creating family memories. Hey, I'm not suggesting your kids are going to immediately love this volunteer thing over a trip to Disney World but guess what? When they are grown, they will look back and remember how mom and dad had a heart to serve others even when things were tough. You will impart lifelong wisdom to your kids through showing by example how to handle life's storms. Also, I think its important to be honest with kids about financial issues at home. This provides better communication and allows kids to feel like trusted individuals in their home.

Using reframing for the worst life experiences

Did you know the brain has a hard time moving on from a negative experience? Let me explain. One of the reasons you might be struggling to come to terms with an unfortunate situation is because you have framed that experience highlighting only the bad things that have happened. Putting a better frame around your story changes the meaning of your bad experience allowing you to see the gain, growth and transformation from it. There is no cookie cutter way to get past a difficult situation, but this will help you to move on from the negative frame and be empowered to create healing and a greater experience.

I want to now share a personal story that ended up being the ultimate test of this technique in my life. It was around 11:30 at night when I got the call that Mom had passed away. I had a two year-old son in the next room and a newborn daughter next to me who would never be able to know their grandmother. Never be able to laugh with her, create fun memories, or have her attend their wedding. They would never be able to witness her brazen acts of wearing whatever she wanted, no matter how ridiculous it looked. I felt the wind leave my chest as I hung up the phone and called my brother and sister to talk about the news we had all dreaded.

We arrived at the nursing home where they took us in the back to see our mom, who was lying on a bed, very still. Her eyes were closed, and she was clutching a set of rosary beads. She wasn't Catholic so we were not sure where those came from. We were each understandably sad; we had just lost both our mother and father in this single death. Years of memories flooded through each of us in the span of seconds. It was like someone turned off the lights in the middle of a performance. We felt lost. We stared at the body of our lifeless mother on that bed for what seemed like an eternity.

I looked over at my brother and sister, and I could tell they were going down a dark rabbit hole of grief. As was I. In that moment, something rose inside of me. I felt it welling up inside my vocal cords, and there was no stopping it. Here comes that inner fighter again. As I looked over at my brother and sister with tear filled eyes, I blurted out, "Wow, looks like she has a death grip on those rosary beads, huh?"

Complete silence.

My brother hung his head and started laughing, and his knees buckled. My sister followed suit putting her hands over her face laughing. My brother chimed in, "And when did she become Catholic?" We laughed even harder. The three of us laughed so uncontrollably that the nurse came back there and asked if we were okay.

Here's what happened:

In what was clearly the saddest day of my life. I remembered who my mom was: her contagious spirit of laughter, her upbeat and fun energy. She always told us, "When I die, I don't want you to feel sad! I want you to be happy knowing I'm with Jesus up in heaven singing songs and riding horses!" (Side note: she *loved* horses.) Strange as it may seem, this was a perfect example of the odd experiences my mom prepared us for. She told us this over and over during our childhood. In that moment, I decided to reframe this very sad situation so that my brother, sister, and I could see it differently. Make no mistake, we were absolutely devastated to lose our mom. I am tearing up as I write about her. It's been 20 years since her death, and I miss her terribly. On the day she passed, I chose a frame that celebrated her life, her mission, and her laughter instead of a frame that told me she was gone.

You get to decide from here on out which frames you want to use in your own life. When you think of a painful experience that happened to you, how will you frame it?

When you think of your divorce, will you frame it with thankfulness to have had some good years with this person and maybe some wonderful, healthy children? Or are you going to frame it with bitterness and resentment because it' didn't turn out the way you hoped?

When you think of a bankruptcy, are you going to frame it with a story that tells you at least you were brave enough to take a chance on a new business, opportunity, or project? Or are you going to frame it with a story that your life is in ruin because you have to start over financially?

I want you to know that life keeps moving whether you play along or not. There is a valuable lesson in everything that happens to us. Almost any negative experience can be reframed to focusing on the transformation, healing or growth instead of the pain. Make a list of three bad situations that have happened to you. Now imagine them with a new frame and write down this new way of seeing it. The more you practice this strategy in your life, the less baggage, hurt feelings and resentment you carry with you. This ultimately gives you more space for love, forgiveness and healing.

Chapter Eleven

Putting The Right Systems In Place

Let's talk

If you're like me, having things organized makes you happier. My closest friends know that I am an organizational freak of sorts. When I walk into the container store, I feel like I've just entered an oasis that only my kind of people can understand. They make the most unbelievable types of containers for everything in your life. If you want to find the perfect container to store your bobby pins, Christmas wrapping paper, spices, socks, etc. You name it and they've got you covered. My obsession with containers is not so much the neat look that you get as a result of the organizational process. Rather, it's the concept of having systems in place for the things in your life that you use every day. Being able to organize them in a meaningful way sends my heart into overdrive. When things are organized, you find them faster, and you have less clutter sitting around your house because everything has a place. You also save time in your day because you're no longer looking for things. Everything is at your fingertips. I know, I know. I'm a special kind of weird and that's okay. Please try not to judge. On second thought, judge away. I'm used to being a little different.

There is a method to my madness. When my outer world is organized, it helps me be calmer, more peaceful, and increases my productivity. I've never been formally diagnosed with Attention Deficit Disorder, but I feel like it's possible that I have it. People with ADD need organization to feel calm. They need structure and a well laid out plan for each task. Some of this might be resonating with you as you read this.

In this chapter, I want to discuss three important systems that have helped me to be more effective:

1. Tips for organizing your day
2. Time management
3. Accountability.

You might be asking what does having systems in place have to do with the the topic of happiness. Well, I'm not sure about you, but having control of my day and time ultimately means more freedom for me to do other stuff that makes me happy. It also means feeling less stress, which is always delightful.

Lessons learned

Organizing your day

And while, yes, I did start this chapter talking about an organizational craze, my overall point is that I want you to start thinking of your day like an area of your home that needs to be organized and have systems in place to be more effective. If you can get in the habit of preparing ahead of time for events as well as grouping similar actionable tasks and then tackling them at the same time, you'll save time, money, and be less stressed.

Here are some examples:

- **Plan your week ahead** - Pick a day/time each week to sit down with your calendar and plan your week ahead. This will take so much stress off you because you can foresee what events, activities, and tasks you need to plan for and if you need to bring or do anything to be prepared ahead of time. This alleviates forgetting important events and it gives you a greater sense of control over your schedule.
- **Stack and attack all errands** - If you have a bunch of errands, use a process called "stack and attack". This means try to group all errands to a certain geographical area. For example: if you need groceries, supplies for your home, a post office and bank run, you could map out a route where all these places might be in the same three-mile radius. I have put off running certain errands to another day if I know I'll be in the same area later in the week. Why make a special trip if it can wait until you are in that area later?
- **Managing phone calls** - Try to return all calls when you are doing something that doesn't require diligent mental aptitude like driving or painting your nails or cleaning your house. Or you could sit still and give the caller your undivided attention, but honestly, my nerves flare up when I even think about doing this. Its hard for me to sit completely still so I find it easier to do certain tasks while I'm also using my motor skills.

> *"A good system shortens the road to the goal."*
> *~ Orison Swett Marden*

Time management

There are only two time management tips that I found to be the most useful. Let's examine both:

A. Best time for mental peak performance

One of the most important things that I can mention about time management is to first figure out what time of the day you are more mentally energized. For myself, it is first thing in the morning, usually between 7AM-10AM. Once you figure out when you are most likely at your mental peak, this is the time slot that you want to reserve for your projects that require you to be the most mentally assertive. I like to use this time for creative writing, planning, and strategizing.

B. Time blocking

Here is something that has helped me with time management and completing tasks. When I have things that I need to do but I know that I might not feel like doing them, I set an alarm clock for a set period to start and stop each task. This is referred to as the "The Pomodoro Technique" I say to myself that I am going to accomplish as much as I can within that designated time and then I will stop. I don't allow myself to answer incoming calls, text messages, or anything that may distract me. I stay focused. Using this method, I can get so much more done and usually with time to spare. I will then reward myself with something I enjoy, like a phone call to a friend for some girl talk, dancing to music, or even a treat like a chocolate croissant. The key is to reward yourself with something you will enjoy. This helps you to stay on task knowing that you are going to get something special once you're finished.

Accountability is a must

Nothing, and I mean nothing, will help you more than having someone hold you accountable for the deadlines that you have set around your goals. You can ask a likeminded friend to help you or a family member. What I've done in the past is I've agreed to be someone's accountability partner in exchange for them being mine, so it's a win-win for both of us. A little piece of advice: please have respect for this person's time. If you make a commitment to have certain things accomplished on a particular day, then make sure you get it done! You want your accountability partner to be proud of you and know that you are taking your goals seriously. Knowing that you must answer to someone else is going to light a fire under you like never before. Just try it and you'll see what I'm talking about! Having accountability is probably one of the smartest things you can ever do for your success!

Chapter Twelve
Creating Killer Habits

Let's talk

I have something embarrassing to share and since I feel like we are slowly becoming friends, I figured this is a safe space to open up about my deepest shortcomings. Here goes: I started writing this book 15 years ago. I know, right? I mean I feel like this book is good but it's not 15 years in the making good. What on earth took me so long to finish it, you ask? It's simple. One distraction led to another distraction, and here we are 15 years later. There's something strangely cathartic about admitting that you have been a horrible procrastinator. Whew, I'm glad I got that off my chest.

I've always been clear about my goals. Like many of you, I write out my goals at the beginning of each year. I work hard to try and achieve them throughout the year, and I can promise you I don't lollygag my time away. I'm an extremely methodical, systems oriented, and results-driven type of personality. I barely watch TV, but somehow 15 years managed to slip away from me. I had to have a real honest come-to-Jesus talk with myself about why this goal of mine was still flapping in the wind. Here's the bottom line: at the time, this goal was not important enough to me. Ouch, it was painful to type that, but it's obviously true. It is now of course, but back then not so much. Maybe you have a goal that you've been wanting to accomplish for a while now, and if you haven't made any progress on it, you might have to admit some hard truths to yourself as well.

In reality, life had me busy raising two kids as a single parent. I was also consumed with buying, rehabbing, and renting out properties to build a financial future for myself and with whatever spare time I had left, I was traveling the world. I know, I know, don't cry for me, Argentina. But seriously, life boils down to choices. Have you asked yourself what is the most important goal for you to accomplish this year?

Lessons learned

I read an incredible book called *Atomic Habits* by James Clear, and it really opened my eyes with respect to building good habits but also breaking the bad ones. So, in full disclosure, most of the remaining content in this chapter will be credited to Clear. He is the hero here. I figured why re-invent the wheel when our man, Clear, has already made so many good points. His book is *amazing*, and if you want a deeper dive into the topic of habits, please go read *Atomic Habits*.

How to develop killer habits

The number one killer of goals is distractions. There is a saying in the Christian world, "If the devil can't make you a bad person, he'll make you a busy person." Meaning, if he can keep you distracted from the goals around your faith, he has already won. The same concept is true when it comes to goal achievement.

When it comes to habits, many people think they lack motivation when they actually lack clarity. Being specific about what you want and how you want to achieve it helps you to say no to any distractions that pop up. Clear writes that, "We say yes to little requests that steal our time because we are not crystal clear about what we should be doing instead." When your dreams are vague, it's easy to be distracted and rationalize the little interruptions all day along. This one really hit me like a ton of bricks!

Clear says that in order for us to take action on our habits, we must have what is called "Implementation Intentions," which is a set of specific plans to implement and take action. It looks like this:

I will [BEHAVIOR] at [TIME] in [LOCATION]

For example:
I will write for 1 hour at 5PM at my local Starbucks.
I will exercise for 30 mins at 7AM in my living room.
I will spend 15 mins each morning at 6:30AM meditating or praying in my dining room.

People who make a specific plan for when and where they will perform a new habit are more likely to follow through. Saying that "I'm going to write more," or "I'm going to eat healthier," are useless because if we never say when and where these habits are going to happen, it's like a car with no gas.

> *"First, forget inspiration. Habit is more dependable. Habit will sustain you whether you're inspired or not."*
> ~ Octavia Butler

Set yourself up for success

We're all motivated differently, but I think most people need simplicity to get started. I have learned that if you want to create a new habit, you need to keep it super simple and easy to repeat. Over time, this will eventually turn into a ritual, and that's when you've won the battle. Clear states that if we want to start a new habit, we should strive to make it achievable in less than two minutes. For example,

- Reading before bed - read one page.
- Do thirty minutes of yoga- start by taking out your yoga mat.
- Run three miles - start by tying your running shoes.

The point is not to accomplish that one thing. The point is to master the habit of showing up. A habit must be established before it can be improved. Sometimes if you think about the result that you want, like running three miles, it can be overwhelming. However, by showing up, you are focusing on the type of person you want to become and not necessarily the result. It's better to play two minutes of the guitar than none. It's better to run for a few minutes than not. It's better to read one page of the book than not reading at all. Make it easy to start, and the rest will follow.

Breaking bad habits

So, what about bad habits? How do we break those bad boys? Well, you burn the bridges. You make it unattractive, reduce exposure, and reframe your mindset. There was a French author named Victor Hugo, who had a propensity to procrastinate on his writing assignments. He had a huge publishing deadline that he was afraid he would not make. So, he had his assistant lock all of his clothing in a chest, so he had nothing to wear outside the house. This kept him indoors writing all winter and he met his publishing deadline two weeks early. We all have bad habits. Maybe it's eating too much junk food, consuming too much social media, gossiping; only you know what yours are.

If you've made a conscious decision that these behaviors are not serving you or are blocking your blessings, you'll want to stop doing them. But how do you do this? You must make your bad habits difficult to do by creating what psychologist's refer to as a "Commitment Device." This blocks you from doing the bad habit. If it's eating junk food, stop buying it at the grocery store so it's not in your pantry for easy consumption. If it's too much social media, you can set a timer to turn off your Wi-Fi at a certain time of night so you can be sure to get proper rest. Figure out what a good commitment device would be for any bad habits.

The importance of a morning routine

Clear points out in his book that if you are having trouble changing your habits, the problem isn't you, the problem is your systems. One of the systems that I've created and absolutely love is a powerful morning routine. This sets the tone for my day and anchors me to a consistent mood. This way it doesn't matter if I'm in a good mood when I wake up or not; my morning routine will automatically put me into a peak mental state. Here is an example of my morning routine:

- Do a 5–15-minute morning devotional (Prayer, read Bible, etc.)
- I turn on uplifting music or listen to an inspirational podcast
- I do green juicing (extract juices from Spinach, Kale, Carrots, Apple, Celery)
- Go to gym and get a great workout
- Review my daily and weekly goals

If you are looking for a good place to start with creating some good habits, I highly recommend starting with a simple morning routine. Use mine as a base and add or takeaway items that are fitting to you and your fancy. Clear is an expert on habits, but I promise you that I have been doing this morning routine for years, and I can fully attest that it works! As you can see, I have a combination of great habits that include nourishment for my physical body and my mental wellbeing. But remember to start small. Do what you can each day until it becomes habit and routine. By doing this, I know you will feel happier, more energized, and anchored to peace throughout your day.

Chapter Thirteen
How To Pull Yourself Out Of A Rut

Let's talk

I am an amazing, motivated, highly energetic, optimistic, and positive person. I can also be negative, glass half empty, want to stay in bed and have a good cry type of gal too. I know what you're thinking: how can I be writing a book and teaching others how to get their happy back if I am admitting to you that I suffer from the same type of negative and limiting beliefs as everyone else? Well then, I'm about to blow your mind.

I have lived through a lot of hardships and learned many lessons. It is the result of those tough experiences that I feel a deep calling in my heart to share the wisdom that I've learned which could help enrich the life of someone else who may be struggling. Thats the good news. The bad news is there are some days when I wake up not feeling my usual upbeat and happy self. Negative and self sabotaging thoughts try to takeover.

Here's the interesting thing about limiting beliefs. They know exactly what area of your life you are working hardest on and that's where they plan their attack. It could be your weight loss/body image journey, your relationship with your partner, the area of your finances to name a few. In my case, it usually has to do with my creativity or journey to help others. Thats the area these negative thoughts start attacking me. Thoughts like "I don't have a degree in Psychology, so who am I to tell people how to live a happier life" or "no one is going to take me seriously because I don't have a huge following on Instagram" or my all time favorite limiting belief is "I'm probably too old to be starting this new venture."

Like many people, when these thoughts come, they are vicious. They can stress me into feeling depressed and before I know it, I might find that I have slipped into a mental rut. Sometimes it can feel like I am being a total fraud if I try to be the happier version of myself because these beliefs are so convincing when you are already feeling low energy. Even though I know these negative thoughts are not true at all, it's extremely frustrating especially when you are trying to create or build something you've never done before. If you've ever experienced limiting beliefs in the area of your business, being creative and exploring something new, or even a job for which you are trying to take on a new position, you are not alone. They call it "imposter syndrome," and this is very common in the beginning stages of expanding yourself and the vision for your life.

This is just one of the many forms of a mental rut that we can find ourselves in. Oh, and by the way, these emotional ruts don't ever give us a heads up that they are on the way. You just wake up, and BAM! It's a new day and a new mental state for you to work through. It can be really tough to pull yourself out of this funk and be productive. And if you're writing a book on how to help others find their happy, it can be quite embarrassing to share something like this, but proudly, here I am.

Lessons learned

I want you to understand that we are all susceptible of having both good days and bad days. That's a part of life that we have to accept whether we like it or not. It does not matter if you are a preacher, doctor, therapist, self-help guru, or an aspiring writer trying to help people find their happy; there is nothing to be ashamed of or embarrassed by if you find yourself in a rut. Like you, I am the sum of all my previous experiences, including the trauma it has left in my life and the moods that I struggle to manage daily.

I want to share a few things that have helped me when I am deep in sadness, feel lost or mentally stuck. Now I want you to promise me something: No matter how silly you think some of these are, I want you to still do them. Because when you are stuck in a rut, your brain will try to convince you that these things are stupid, silly, and they won't work. Just a heads up that your brain can lie to you. Our brains are designed to keep us alive, not to make us happy. Back in ancient times, our brains had to be on high alert to notify us of dangerous animals that could eat us. Because of this evolutionary design, we are prewired to have a negative disposition of always looking for the problem or what is wrong within our lives. We have to re-program our mind to serve us in todays world. It can be a fight each day for some of us to get and stay happy. So do not beat yourself up if you are feeling sadness, just get up and do some of these things because they work!

> "When you've exhausted all possibilities, remember this: You haven't."
> ~ Thomas Edison

Physical movement

It is nearly impossible to stay in a depressed mental state if you are moving your body and working up a sweat. Hence the term "motion changes emotion." I have tried this and it really works! Have you ever seen an angry person riding a bicycle? I'm pretty sure it's impossible. So, if you are able to get up and move your body; try changing your physical state first and your emotional state will follow. You can take a nice leisurely walk outside and get some fresh air. And while you're taking your walk and enjoying the beautiful great outdoors, you can listen to your favorite podcast or uplifting music. Doing physical movement to something that feeds or inspires your brain is a great combination to feel better!

Pray, forgive, and release

I don't know what your faith is, but prayer or talking to your Higher Power is a great place to surrender the things that are bothering you. Prayer has been a beautiful practice with many benefits in my life. Our God/Source Creator wants us to talk to Him about everything that is in our hearts. I have cried my heart out to God during some of the challenging seasons in my life. It feels so good to talk directly to my Creator and share the disappointments of my human experience on tough days. I share when I'm feeling lost, sad, heartbroken and ask for His comforting grace.

I also open my heart to share with Him whenever I feel inadequate or confused in certain situations. I ask that He give me support and divine wisdom in these areas. Here is a quick little prayer that has helped me when I feel anger or resentment towards another. You can say this little prayer regardless of your religious beliefs. Think of the person who may have hurt you and say:

"I forgive (say the person's name) and release with love to the Holy Spirit/Universe."

This prayer is so powerful and comforting at the same time because it frees you from carrying around hurt feelings. You are now free to live your life without being attached to resentment, anger, or revenge, which only weigh you down like a ton of bricks.

Write your feelings in a journal

If prayer doesn't fit you, another therapeutic way to get your feelings out can be to write them down in a journal. If a person has hurt you, try writing a letter to them but never send it. Tell them how they made you feel, how their actions may have changed your viewpoints on love, friendship or life. Get your anger out. Give yourself permission to write anything you want! You can even draw pictures, use colored markers, and highlighters. Get creative and honor your feelings because you matter.

Laugh it out

One of my favorite ways to snap out of a funk is to laugh my butt off. I have the free edition of Pandora, and I listen to the Dave Chapelle and Daniel Tosh stations. They have a decent rotation of similar comedians, and the content always snaps me out of my mood and makes me laugh. Comedy is simply a different perspective, a funny way of seeing things. I've heard comedian's joke about topics that you would never in a million years think would be funny, but they are crafty. It's refreshing to be pulled into another person's world, especially when they are using humor.

Another thing that has worked extremely well for me especially during the pandemic of 2020 was the app Tik Tok. If you don't know what this is, you should download it! Basically, you have average people like you and me doing funny skits, sharing way too personal stories, or making fun of themselves. There has not been one time that I've logged in that I didn't spend at least 20 minutes on the app laughing. The Tik Tok community are incredibly talented and funny. Also, they have doctors and other professionals on there that teach you all kinds of stuff ranging from relationship issues, medical topics, exercise videos, etc. It's the best app ever to cheer you up, and you will even learn some cool things, too!

Be around people

Okay, I realize this one may be tough if you are feeling depressed. The last thing you want to do is be around people, smile, and act normal when you just want to cry into your pillow. The mind will want you to pull away to a dark place when you are hurt. That's why I left this one for last. My hope for you is that once you have tried the previous suggestions, you can work your way into a better state and get out amongst the living again. I promise if you can force yourself to get back out there, you will realize that life is worth living. We all have problems we are struggling with but being around people reminds us that we are not alone. I know it might sound crazy to say this, but we need each other.

I recommend doing something that you enjoy to start out with. If you like dancing, sign up for a dance class. Maybe you like karaoke - go sing until your heart is content. Or maybe you don't mind rolling up to a bar and having a drink. This one is tough for me because I don't drink, and I feel incredibly shy and out of place at a bar, like everyone is staring at me. However, I am happy to report that at the time of this writing, I have forced myself recently to go to a bar by myself. I wanted to get out and meet more people, and I challenged myself to do it. I highly recommend you push yourself out of your comfort zone when you're ready. But *only* when you're ready. Baby steps.

I hope you have enjoyed this chapter. I almost didn't include it because I didn't want this Principle to have too many chapters. But how could I possibly write a book about how to get your happy back and not tell you guys how to pull yourselves out of a rut?

Principle #5

Learn To Pivot

In this Principle, we will be discussing how to improvise, adapt, and overcome

- Be open to change

- Finding your purpose or passion

- Reinventing yourself after life's curve balls

LET'S GET STARTED!

Chapter Fourteen
Be Open To Change

Let's talk

I hate change. If you come back with the wrong type of milk, we're going to have a sit-down about it. Okay, maybe I'm over exaggerating. Or am I? Anyways, change is not easy for some of us. A big thief of happiness can be expecting things to turn out one way in your life, and when they turn out differently, you might associate it with failure. But what if you're wrong? What if it's not a failure at all? What if it's the universe trying to redirect your steps to something bigger and better? If you are open to change, you will see these opportunities when they come up. Conversely, if you are closed to change and can only see things as being one way, you might be missing out on something wonderful.

Years ago, I wanted to pursue acting. I had always lived in the Washington DC/Maryland area. Unfortunately, back then most of the acting jobs were in Los Angeles or New York. I went back and forth to New York several times for auditions, but nothing panned out. I took acting classes when I could, and I eventually secured small parts in local theater and a couple of roles in some low budget movies. I never officially closed the door to acting, but life got in the way.

I got married, had two children, and settled into being a great mother and wife. As it turns out, my marriage ended as many unfortunately do. I found myself raising my two kids as a single parent while also trying to support myself, and it wasn't easy. Nothing ever goes as planned. That's how life is.

After the dust settled in my personal life, I continued to work in real estate to support myself. It gave me the flexibility I needed to be with my kids when they got home from school. I also started to revisit my dream of acting. I had new headshots done, went to acting expos and signed up for acting classes again. I traveled back and forth on the 5-hour bus ride to and from New York going to audition after audition. It was hard. I was denied roles because my hair was too long, I was too tall, or too sexy looking for the motherly roles that were appropriate to my age. It was always something. The rejection factor was incredibly high. Trying to work full time, pursue my acting dream while also being a single mom, was taking its toll. I'd work a long day then come home, make dinner, and help the kids with their homework. After they went to bed, I'd return emails from clients, search for new auditions and prepare headshots, Tidy up the house and pass out in bed. Talk about insane!

> *"Life is either a daring adventure or nothing at all..."*
> *~ Helen Keller*

I have the spirit of a fighter by nature in that I don't just give up easily on things. I had to be tough growing up and maybe that's where my tenacity comes from. I didn't want to give up my dream of pursuing acting but I was feeling deeply discouraged. This wasn't the first time that I had tried to pursue acting, and I didn't want to quit. But the rejection remains tough time after time. I began praying and asking God for guidance. I didn't know what else to do. I honestly didn't feel that I could do any more to become an actor short of moving to New York or LA. That was simply not an option for me. I was sharing custody of my two amazing kids with their father. However, it seemed as though if I wanted to make a go of this acting thing, it would require me to move away without them. There was just NO WAY I would ever leave my kids behind for anything! I'm sure a lot of parents can relate.

This was a moment of clarity for me. I knew I had this creativity inside me that was screaming to get out, a deep-seated desire to perform or create something. I didn't know what or how. I thought it was acting, but boy, was that not working out as planned. I couldn't help but feel there had to be some way that I could express my creative side to satisfy this inner desire but also still be present to raise my children. This is the biggest challenge for a lot of parents. We love our children, but how do we still go after our dreams?

Lessons learned

Something inside me shifted. I knew there had to be more than one way to express myself creatively and I was going to find it. One day it dawned on me that I had been through so many interesting things in life. Starting from early childhood, being homeless many times, putting myself through college, buying my first investment property at 17 years old. Not to mention getting married then divorced, starting over financially and ultimately obtaining financial freedom before 40 years old. Not only did I survive all of these obstacles, but I always found the strength to push myself towards something greater. I kept going and maximized every opportunity all while maintaining a spirit of happiness and joy. That's when a light bulb went on: I could do something with all these experiences to help other people. I could share what I learned, encourage others, and inspire people to dig deep and go after the life they deserve. Yes, acting had always been a dream of mine, but the truth is I've always had a huge burning desire to make a difference in this world.

I started researching the best way to help others while exploring my own creativity. I read countless personal development books over the years, but my passion to learn more was reignited. I traveled to attend a bunch of workshops and seminars. I networked with lots of new people who had this same passion in their hearts so we could encourage and inspire each other. This was a whole new world for me, and I became relentless about figuring out how I could bridge the gap from where I currently was to where I wanted to be. If you are reading this book, it's because you have a desire in your heart to be, do, or have more than what your current life is giving you. In the same way that I shifted from one path to a new one, I know that you can do the same!

Of course, I was scared and nervous. I thought to myself, "Why would anyone want to listen to me? I'm not as smart or as accomplished as some of the other leaders in the space I was trying to enter." But that's just a lie that we tell ourselves out of fear! We all have something to offer, and we each have our own unique energetic signature and perspective on life experiences to share with others. I heard once that God would not have given us a dream in our heart if He didn't also give us the ability to achieve it. You are incredibly different than anyone else and you have your own individual talents to bring to the table.

When you can embrace this idea, that's when you begin to fly and reach your full potential in life. I've always told my kids, "'Don't be afraid to be different". I enjoy pulling away from the pack and being my own unique person. Who cares what anyone else thinks? I told them that if two people are the same, one of them is unnecessary. It's true. So, you might as well be different and live an authentic life.

I am still researching the opportunities that can bring me closer to realizing my dream of helping others. I know now that acting was simply one form of creativity. I can be creative in other ways like public speaking, writing books, putting on charity fashion shows, and many more exciting things. The possibilities are endless. I don't have to limit myself, and neither do you! We don't have to allow ourselves to feel like a failure because the one path we started on didn't work out. Keep your heart and mind open for new possibilities!

Be scared, but do it anyway

Is there a dream sitting deep within your heart, waiting to come out? A yearning to do something bold and different? I bet there is, or you wouldn't be here reading these words. I know what that feels like. Perhaps you might be scared to go after that dream because you feel that it's too over the top or unreachable. Maybe you've tried to talk yourself out of it a thousand times, but the urge refuses to go away. You are still curious about it and I think thats beautiful! I believe that you owe it to yourself to see what potential lies within you.

Or maybe you did go after that dream, but it didn't pan out like in my case. Please don't let that discourage you from trying something new. Get creative to see how you can get going with something else. Don't ever give up! Like what happened to me, you can start out going after one dream and realize that your original idea was just a steppingstone to get you to your ultimate life's purpose. Helping other people realize their potential is far more rewarding to me than playing any role in the acting field. Who knows what the future holds for you too! Remember this: your detour can lead to your destiny! I hope the content in this chapter gives you the permission to take that first step towards exploring your heart's dream.

Chapter Fifteen
Finding Your Purpose Or Passion

Let's talk

It's okay if you don't have your whole life figured out yet. Let me share a little secret with you: most people don't. The way to figure it out is to keep momentum. Keep searching, reading, asking yourself questions, and moving in a direction, even if you are not certain. Sometimes you need to stop and reevaluate your goals. Are you really on the right track? Are you really going after the things that matter most in your life? Maybe you need to reassess your core values. At the end of your days, what is the most important thing to have accomplished in your life before you leave this planet? What do you want to be remembered for? I guarantee that if you take the time to answer some of these questions, you will gain clarity.

I used to rack my brain trying to figure out what my passion was. What was I good at? What was my purpose in life? I've heard that if you find your passion, something you are truly good at, then you will find your purpose. Well, let me tell you that I read books. Lots of books. I took all those fancy "passion tests," looking to find answers. I realized after years of searching that I had it all wrong. That's because you can't cognitively discover your passion through an intellectual scavenger hunt. Passions are born out of experiences. Remember when you cried during a movie? It's because of how that movie made you feel through watching the story unfold before your eyes. Remember the feelings of nostalgia that you felt after hearing a song that brought back memories of an experience or of someone that you loved? It's because the emotions were solicited through that listening experience. Another way to further explain this is if you enjoy certain physical activities, like biking. You enjoy this experience because of the beautiful scenery you see, the feeling of the crisp breeze on your cheeks as it rushes past your face and ears, or the feeling of the adrenaline rush knowing that you are challenging your body's physical limits and getting into better shape.

> *"It is in the act of creating new experiences that we discover who we are."*
>
> *~ Anonymous*

These are all examples of experiences that left a mark on you. The emotions you felt, the passion that you had, all came *after* the initial experience, not before. Discovering your passion in life and in work will follow that same pattern. I've never found a burning passion for something while sitting on the sofa. If we want to discover what our inner passion might be, we need to get in motion and create a sparking experience. We need to research new ideas, make new or different choices, and push ourselves out of our comfort zone to try new things. It is in the act of creating new experiences that we discover who we are.

If you have been searching for your passion and haven't found it yet, what makes you think that you will find it by doing the same routine? You must change it up. You must change your actions to change your outcome. If you want a *new* passion, you must create a *new* experience.

Lessons learned

Is there someone that is living a life you admire? There is a saying that if you want to be successful, all you need is to find someone who is doing what you want to do and copy them. Do what they do, and you can be successful just like them. You may think that someone else is more talented than you, and that's why they have a better life than you. This is untrue. Michael Jordan once said, "Anyone can have talent, but ability takes hard work". I know people who only have the gift of being able to work hard, and guess what? They are successful! Success means different things to different people. I urge you to find someone who is living the life you want and study them. How do they make their money? If it's a lifestyle that you want, exactly what is it that you admire? Define it. Break it down. They found a way to their success, and you can, too.

What you like versus what you know

Some people think that you should start with what you know. I disagree. If you can't find your passion using what you already know, why would you stick with that method? I'm not suggesting that you throw away the skills you've learned. Feel free to use your knowledge base but use those skills to create new experiences. Try not to choose a career path simply because it's something that you feel comfortable doing. Your choices should be based on what you like, not what you know. However, don't confuse liking something for being passionate about it. Your liking may eventually turn into a passion, but for now, it is simply an interest that you are exploring.

Another way to getting closer to our passion, or life's calling if you will, is to dedicate yourself to a cause, something that serves or helps others. This has been proven to be effective and helpful for many because what can be better than serving others? In addition to the rewarding benefit of helping another, this process helps you to gain a new experience that you otherwise may not have had.

How goals can lead us to our passion

When you seek out a new experience, you will automatically be creating a new set of goals for yourself. Say, for example, you want to take a cooking class. You want to feel what it's like to learn about nutrition and creating well-balanced meals. Your goal might be researching where to take these classes. Another goal might be to reorganize your kitchen so that you can function better when preparing your meals. Sometimes it is the process of achieving these smaller goals that we grow and find our passion. What do I mean? The value of having a goal and pursuing new experiences can be as much a part of our journey as the accomplishment of reaching the goal itself. The experiences we have, the lessons we learn, and the doors it opens are all part of what brings us closer to finding our passion. We cannot possibly predict where a journey will take us or what it will reveal. We can only start the journey and let things evolve naturally. The pursuit will bring it to us.

But I have so many interests, how do I choose?

I've talked with people who have told me they have lots of different dreams in their heart. They will say that their interests are so diverse and that they can't choose only one. But here's the thing: you need to start somewhere. You can't allow yourself to make excuses like this, which will cripple you mentally until you end up not doing anything.

Here's what you do in this situation: Make a list of all your interests and be sure to number them by order of how much you're interested in them. Next, pick the one at the top of the list, and try that for as long as it takes.

Either one or two things will happen:
(1.) You will eventually get tired of it, bored, or lose interest.
(2.) It will ignite a flame in your heart that you cannot put out. You will wake up each morning and jump out of bed ready to tackle the next obstacle because you know that this is something you *must* continue.

Here's how the process works: Once you pick the first thing you want to explore, you will have to set goals around this new project to make any progress. We've already discussed earlier how to set goals in a way that it will help you stay focused and on track. If you're afraid that you will lose interest too quickly without giving the proper time and effort, don't be too hard on yourself. This is something that a lot of people struggle with. What you want to do is go back and read the principle on forming amazing habits. There are excellent strategies in there to help you create killer habits and stay focused.

Is this my true passion?

A lot of people ask me, "How will I know when I have found my passion?" This is a very good question. Think of it like this: You're not looking for "passion" or a "calling." What you are really looking for is a moment, a moment when you say to yourself, "This is right. This is where I am supposed to be and what I am supposed to be doing. Right here, right now, this is what I am meant to do." You don't find moments like this, they find you through experiences.

When we dedicate ourselves to creating new experiences, trying new things, and setting goals, these moments find us more often. Finding our passion is not about knowing with certainty that we have chosen the right direction. It's about picking a direction and pursuing it with urgency and enthusiasm. When we do this, it's another way that experiences can bring our passion to us.

You're never too old

If you haven't gotten around to starting the business you've always wanted, please don't fall into the mind trap of thinking you are too old. You are never too old to go after something important to you. Matter of fact, most business founders are around the age of 40 when they get started. Sam Walton, the founder of Walmart didn't begin having massive success until after age 44. Maybe its not the business world that tickles your fancy. Maybe you want to venture into the creative arts and become a writer, actor, singer. Just know that most people don't have success in these areas either until later in life. Samuel L. Jackson didn't land his first award winning acting role until the age of 43. Vera Wang who is arguably one of the world's top fashion designers used to be a figure skater and journalist before entering the fashion industry at age 40.

The truth is we are never too old to start living life to the fullest. We should be living our life to the fullest right now! Let's not wait for tomorrow! If there is something you have been dreaming of doing, you should plan and do it now. You don't want to look back and have a life of regrets!

Chapter Sixteen

Reinventing Yourself After Life's Curve Balls

Let's talk

Life is always going to throw you curve balls that knock you down. At the beginning of this book, I shared with you one of my earliest curve balls, which was the rejection of my father's love. I managed to pick myself up and carved out a nice life for myself, then another curve ball came: my daughter almost died a week after she was born. She came down with Respiratory Syncytial Virus and had to be hospitalized for several days in intensive care. A week later, my mother died. I had a newborn baby one week, and the next week, I was cremating my mother who was my everything. I picked myself back up only to have another curve ball come: my marriage fell apart. These are just a few of my hard times, and I'm sure you have had some devastating ones, too. But God didn't allow it to break you or me because we are still here fighting to become better. I want you to know that those times are not going to stop coming for us. So, we might as well get better at learning how to keep going, each time getting stronger and smarter. If I can do it, trust me, I know you can, too!

I've met women who struggle with bouncing back after a major life setback, and that is why I feel called to write this book, especially this chapter. The biggest issue I've seen is that we convince ourselves that somehow this time is different. This chapter of life hits harder and deeper. We'll say things to ourselves like, "I'm older now, so it's too difficult to bounce back at my age." Listen, guys, these are all lies our brain is telling us because it wants to protect us from starting over. Starting over can be super scary and uncertain, and the brain is doing its job by trying to keep you away from something that it fears might not work out for you. But here's the big question: what if it *does* work out? What if starting over is more beautiful than you ever imagined? What if pushing yourself to learn something that you've never done before launches you into meeting new people, new friends, new opportunities that you never thought possible? What if, by starting over, you end up in a better financial position because you took the leap of faith by starting your own business or going back to school to get a better paying job? The possibilities are endless when you give yourself permission to just go forward.

There is a significant correlation between your levels of happiness and your ability to be self-aware. It's important to pay attention to the things in your life that bring you happiness and the areas where you are barely getting by or silently suffering. You must believe that you are worthy of happiness in your mind and heart before you can see it in your reality. Focusing on the life you want is a great catalyst for reinventing yourself.

Lessons learned

When I was younger, I heard older women say, "Getting old sucks." Now that I'm older, 49 to be exact, I totally understand what they mean, but I respectfully disagree. To me, age is a mindset. I've met women in their 70s who are so full of vitality and life. If you think you are old, you are. If you keep walking around saying that you're old, you will believe it and start acting like it. Your body will agree with you and before you know it; you will start to have joint issues and back pain and any other ailment that you believe is associated with getting older. Stop it! Just stop that way of thinking right now!

Back in my early 30s, I read a book by the late comedian, Joan Rivers. The book was called *Don't Count the Candles, Just Keep the Fire Lit*. Rivers talks about how when she turned 50, she dreaded it and thought that it was the worst thing that could ever happen to her. She felt washed up, over the hill, and not as valuable as the younger women according to society or the entertainment industry she was in. That is until she turned 60-years-old, and she says she would have given anything to be 50 again. The point is to embrace every single age to which you are lucky enough to live.

Listen, none of us can stop the aging process of our body, but we have full control of the aging of our mind. If you are sitting in your house and lamenting the idea of getting older each passing year, it's because you are not making fun a priority in your life. You have too much free time on your hands! I want to challenge you to change that because I know this might be shocking for you to hear, but we are all going to die at some point. Yep, I've read to the end of the book and sorry to inform you, but none of us make it out alive. And since no one is going to come and rescue you, you better stand up and start living right now. Let's make it our mission to squeeze every ounce of juice out of this orange of a life! Okay that was corny, but you get the point.

> *"The secret of change is to focus all of your energy not on fighting the old, but on building the new"*
>
> ~ Socrates

What if I feel discouraged?

When resistance hits, we have two choices: to break down or to break open. Life is always going to be uncertain. When it goes in our favor we rejoice, when it goes against our desires we have trained ourselves to suffer. Remember how earlier I mentioned that nothing has meaning except the meaning we give it? Well, I want to challenge you to think of pain differently from this moment on. Did you know that pain is the single factor that most influences us spiritually? If you have gone through or are going through a tough time right now, just know that pain leads to choices. You will either move toward your spiritual values and seek ways to grow from this experience or look for ways to numb and avoid it. Pain is a great teacher in that it lights the path to important life lessons, provides a deeper sense of our life's purpose, and offers greater clarity on what we most value.

What if my heart is broken?

I know this can be hard. When your heart is broken, it can be tough to get out of bed let alone try to focus on the future. I wish I could impart on you what a beautiful gift pain can be if you embrace it and lean into it. I'll share with you that I am struggling with heartbreak as I'm writing this book. I was dating someone, and the relationship ended. My heart is heavy, and I'd be lying if I said it didn't hurt. Even though I know it's for the best, and I trust God to lead my path forward in a more fulfilling direction, it still hurts. When you release attachment to blaming someone for the pain you feel, even if they were the trigger for it, the experience of pain changes. It becomes something to face head on and learn from. It becomes an opportunity to act on what truly matters rather than continuously struggling to control or avoid it.

I am using this time to dig deeper into myself and my goals, and you should, too. There is a certain clarity that can only be reached when we are hollowed out through pain. As crazy as it seems, there's something so beautiful about being broken wide open with heartache. You have nothing to lose and everything to gain by finding your truest and most raw self. When I say lean in, what I'm referring to is try asking yourself, "why is this happening FOR me? What new perspective can I gain from this situation? What do I need to learn, change, or transform within myself?" Be patient with yourself and the answers will come. Don't rush this process. Go back and read the chapter on self-love mastery and ways to care for and be gentle with yourself during this healing process. Just remember that a broken heart is an open heart. I want you to make it a priority to clean the chambers of your heart so that you can be once again open to giving and receiving love.

Whatever you do, NEVER hold onto bitterness. Learn to forgive and release. If you can't forgive and forget, pick one. The point being don't let holding onto anger and hurt feelings rott you from the inside. Lastly, when you can learn to mentally shift and use your pain as fuel to help you grow towards your goals, you my sweet friend have won.

How do I reinvent myself?

The first step is to decide what needs to be changed in your life. Perhaps there are areas of your life that you are not happy about, but you don't even know where to begin to make changes. Maybe you are afraid that if you make these changes, you might somehow let people down or cause them to be upset with you. Please, forgive me for being sassy here, but I say who gives a crap what anyone else thinks? This is your life! You deserve to be happy however you reinvent yourself for your next chapter.

I have reinvented myself many times over the years. I was once young and single. My time was all mine. I stayed out late, I met new people, I worked hard, saved money, and planned for my future. I put myself through college. I then married and had two children. I reinvented myself. I now shared my time. I gave up my career and depended on my husband to care for us. It was scary for me to depend on someone else financially, but this is the decision we made so I could stay home and raise our children. My new priority was my family. Then I got divorced. I reinvented myself again. Learned how to co-parent with my ex. Started dating again, got into a new relationship. Then my kids grew up and went off to college. Found myself being an empty nester and single once more. Y'all want me to keep going? I sold our family home, moved to another state where I didn't know anyone and started a brand new chapter of life thus reinventing myself yet again. And so much more because life continues to go on.

The point here is that as my circumstances have changed, I had to change to keep up. It is never too late to explore new possibilities for yourself. Reassess where you are right now in your life with respect to your career, your income, your relationships, your health. If you don't like where you are in your life or if you are not happy in any of those areas; you must change it. Don't let anyone ever guilt you into staying in a job that you don't like or a relationship that brings you pain just for the sake of counting years on a calendar. There is no grand award in heaven for years married if you are miserable and hate each other. The reward you get is the time spent together so if you're not enjoying that time with each other, it's time to renegotiate, get counseling or get out. You must do what is best for you. Always. This is your journey through life, and you deserve to live it fully!

Trust yourself enough to wonder

You are capable of so much more than you know if you allow yourself to wonder, to dream, and to explore. Trust yourself enough to be bold and courageous to see what new options could be awaiting you. It's time to start giving yourself permission to try new things. Learn to be sexy again if that's what you want. Try new outfits that make you feel amazing and add spice to your wardrobe. Pay attention to whatever it is inside of you that wants to come out. If you have been through a divorce or a breakup, maybe this is your season to rediscover yourself. Put yourself out there to let the world know you have a vacant position, and you are ready to start taking new applications! If you've been let go from your job, maybe this is the season to wake up and take a risk before it's too late. Start that new business you've been dreaming of. Let your community both in real life and online know that you are ready to serve their needs!

Figure out what makes you happy. Let me show you how. Get out a piece of paper, and write down all the things you've wanted to try or learn. Take the top 3 items and write each item on its own separate piece of paper. Then write down all the ways you can go about making this item happen. For example, if you have always wanted to travel, write this at the top of a blank page. Underneath it, you would list the different places you wanted to go and all the steps necessary to get this ball rolling. For example:

Traveling is my dream

1) I want to travel to South of France, Positano, Italy, Spain.
2) Get online and research some travel groups (so I don't have to travel alone).
3) Research cost of each trip.
4) Start budgeting for first trip - I need to save (fill in $$$ here) per month until (fill in date) I'll be ready to travel.
5) See if I can find someone to travel with who can help share cost to make it more affordable.
6) Find someone to watch my dog.
7) Research medical insurance while abroad.
8) Research international calling plans.
9) Be sure to stop all mail at post office.
10) HAVE FUN, BABY!

And if you really want to take all this to the next level, go back to the chapter on goal-setting and apply the SMART goal method (Specific, Measurable, Attainable, Realistic, Time Specific) to each of these items. You'll be on fire in no time to achieve your dream trips! Use this method for any idea or future projects.

Get involved

Get involved in a group of likeminded people who support you, encourage you, and inspire you. I highly recommend this if you are serious about reinventing yourself. Other strong people show us what's possible. Their boldness is infectious to our spirit. This is just one small example: when you see another woman wearing a bold outfit, there's a part of you that thinks, "hmmm maybe I could look good in that, too." The same thing is true when you are around women who are adventurous. If you see a woman who is fearless and goes hang gliding, jet skiing, rides motorcycles, or jumps out of airplanes, you might think to yourself, "hmmm maybe I could try that." Who knows? You might end up having the time of your life! Come hang with me online for some big sis energy, and yes, I might just have done all of these!

Maybe you are more conservative and don't want to wear bold outfits or do adventurous things, but perhaps you've been curious about making more money. Surround yourself with strong, female business leaders. Look into the Chamber of Commerce groups or join meet-up groups. Get on social media and type in keywords like #femalebizowners #bossbabes #femaleentreprenuer. I'm sure you can easily find them. Ask them questions, buy their books, or take their courses if they offer them. If you want to make more money, you must learn from someone who is doing it. This will cut your learning time in half!

Let go of certainty

If you're like me, you crave certainty. It's how I'm built, but I am learning to let that expectation go. Because the goal is not to become more certain but to surrender into not knowing what will come next. When you turn things over to your Creator/Higher Power, a faithful wisdom appears within you that surpasses control and certainty. My hope is that you will discover what you are capable of and put yourself out there and receive what is yours! Remember, most answers reveal themselves through "doing" and not thinking. Lastly, do not let go of what is precious in life. That is your ability to decide today, that you can reinvent yourself at any age, because you are worthy of having joy and happiness!

Principle #6

Level Up

In this Principle, we will be discussing how to take it to the next level!

- Develop key relationships

- Stop playing small

- Reach back to help others

LET'S GET STARTED!

Chapter Seventeen
Develop Key Relationships

Let's talk

When I was growing up, my mother used to tell me not to hang around the "wrong crowd". Well, I assumed the wrong crowd meant drug dealers, gang members, and thieves. In my late teens, I managed to avoid two out of three. When you're young, you don't place judgement so easily on your friends. Aside from the fact that my boyfriend was a drug dealer, I thought I was still doing okay because he wasn't caught up in a gang or stealing stuff. I was so young and naïve. Make that stupid. But honestly, I always felt safe around him. He carried a gun, which was a 9MM Glock, and people respected him everywhere we went. Back then, I thought that was hot. I was not thinking at all, though I may have already mentioned that. As I grew older, I subconsciously measured the worth of my friendships by the ridiculous barometer that if they weren't selling drugs, stealing, or hurting people then there wasn't any real harm in hanging out with them. Dumb, dumb, and dumb. This type of mindset concerning your friendships can set you back in life.

As I got older, I made the conscious decision to only surround myself with smart and likeminded people. When you are among high achievers, you will eventually become one of them. This is because people who are successful think and talk and behave in a certain way. Their way of thinking inevitably rubs off on you. You witness how they solve problems and how they mentally process challenges that come their way. People who are successful follow a consistent path and have a more positive attitude. They are goal-oriented by nature.

They value their time, are disciplined, and focused. You become who you hang around because you participate in the same activities as your friends. If they have goals, you will want to have goals, too. If your friends are buying nice houses and fancy cars, you will want the same things. You will start to ask yourself: "How can I have nice things in life, too?" Remember, the better questions you ask yourself, the better answers you will receive. If your friends are all successful and you are not, one of two things will eventually happen; you will rise to their level by becoming a more disciplined person and setting goals and working harder. If not, you may find over time that you don't seem to have as much in common and you end up spending less time together.

Lessons learned

Its been said that the success you have in your life will be the average of the five people you associate with the most. This means that if you take the five people you hang around the most and average all their salaries, that will more than likely be the salary that you end up making. Hence the phrase, "Your network is your net worth". Here's the fascinating part: it can also apply to relationships, too. If you are married or are in a relationship, and you hang around friends who are unhappily married or miserable in their relationship, guess what? Your own relationship may begin to suffer. The more you hear your friends complaining about how unhappy they are with their spouse or significant other, you want to be careful that you don't subconsciously begin to pick apart your relationship and find every fault, whether justified or not.

Building quality friendships

How do you know what kinds of people you should have around you? And where do you find them? After all, this is not something we are taught in school. When you were growing up, you probably met and became friends with people that you bumped into at school, at a party, or were introduced to by other friends. But as we get older, it's harder to meet quality people on the whim. Just ask anyone who is single and looking for their life partner. Joining a dating service or trying to meet that right person can seem like a full-time job.

Finding quality friendships is no different. They don't happen by chance, either. I decided to write this chapter because this concept gets overlooked. Let me clarify what I mean by "friends." I'm not referring to casual acquaintances. I'm referring to the people you let into your inner circle. The people you share your wins and losses with. You must consciously choose who to spend your time with. Next to energy, your time is the most precious commodity you have. Yes, even more precious than money. If you lose money, you can always earn more. But once you spend your time, it's gone forever. You can never get it back. Today, I look at forming friendships like forming a business partnership and you should, too. Below are some questions to help guide you with this process:

- What interesting things does this person bring to the table that I can learn from?
- Is this person trustworthy and loyal?
- Could this person give me honest feedback without tearing me down?

- Is this person doing well in managing their own life?
- Is this person goal-oriented or do they have a wasteful use of time?
- Does this person have a growth mindset? Are they always curious and looking for ways to become better?
- Do they give back and serve others in some way?

These are important questions that you need to ask yourself when considering giving someone access to you. It can be fun and comfortable to hang out with people, but if you want to go further faster in life, you may want to purposely seek allied relationships.

Building a power team

No one does it alone. Behind every successful person is usually a team of people who helped encourage, teach, or support their accomplishments in some way. I call these people your power team. A power team is a core group of friends who want you to succeed and are willing to help you do just that.

A power team consists of the following types of people:

- A good listener. They will listen to your challenges and give you constructive feedback.
- An honest person. They will be respectfully honest and tell you what you need versus what you want to hear.
- Someone successful. It doesn't matter what they do if they are successful at it; you can learn from them.
- Someone who is smarter than you. There is a saying that if you are the smartest one among your friends, you need new friends.

> "Your outlook upon life, your estimate of yourself, your estimate of your values is largely colored by your environment. Your whole career will be modified, shaped, molded by your surroundings, by the character of the people with whom you come in contact everyday."
> ~ Orison Swett Marden

Create healthy boundaries

Sometimes we hang around certain people because they are more fun. They bring out a side of us that no one else can. I'm not suggesting that you cut yourself off from these friends and run towards anyone who can help you get ahead in some way. However, you must have your power team intact before you spend time with these other people. Now that you know that your network of friends has a huge impact on your overall net worth, you should be careful as to how much time you spend outside your power team. The reason is that you end up becoming the company you keep. Nothing influences your decisions and your behavior more than the people you are around. Energy is contagious! The energy that you allow around you will influence your motivation, your drive, and your self-esteem. Please, take this seriously. This is something you really need to consider. I want you to learn how to set healthy boundaries by being selective as to who you allow to have access to you.

Chapter Eighteen
Stop Playing Small

Let's talk

Playing small is when you dismiss what you truly want to settle for short term temporary satisfaction. By contrast, playing big means you are willing to experience short term discomfort, uncertainty or risk to go after what you want and deserve.

There were many instances in my life where I was at a cross roads of having to make a tough decision. When I wanted to start a career in real estate investing, it seemed impossible while raising two little kids and also going through a divorce. Years later when my kids went off to college I wanted to sell most of my belongings as well as our family home and downsize to a condo that happened to be a thousand miles away in a state where I didn't know anyone.

These decisions I made were filled with uncertain outcomes, but I challenged myself to step into what I knew I wanted no matter how scary at the time. Playing small means our decisions are motivated by fear. When you play big you are motivated by what brings you true fulfillment and a sense of deep satisfaction. You want to feel more alive and are willing to go for it in the areas you might ordinarily be scared to take that giant leap.

Lessons learned

I know it can be hard to play big when you are met with resistance especially if you are a recovering people pleaser like me. No one knows what is best for you more than you do. That's a true statement. You must stop asking for permission to be yourself. You need to stop caring more about what other people think of your dream. You are allowed to pursue your dreams even if others don't understand it. You're allowed to take time away from your kids and family to push for something more, even if those closest to you don't like it or are inconvenienced by it. You are allowed to tell people who you are and what your needs are instead of concerning yourself if they are going to be "okay" with it first. You don't have to play small in life so others around you don't feel uncomfortable. I've seen people forgo their dreams out of fear of not being loved or accepted by their partners. What are you doing? Stop it! Dream big. Then hit the gas pedal and go even farther! This is your life and your time to show yourself what you are made of. Be the kind of person who shows up for themselves. Be someone who will make a difference in this world in your own way. Be someone bold and unapologetic about what others will think of you. Be the person who can look back when they're 85 years old and think to yourself, "I took the risks, I fell but I got back up. I took a chance on myself, and I'm so glad I did!"

Criticism versus feedback

I want to take a moment and talk about criticism because like the sneaky undertow of seeking permission, this is another way that we unknowingly play small and hand over the reins of our happiness. There is a distinct difference between criticism and feedback. Criticism focuses primarily on the problem without offering any type of practical solution. It can leave you feeling deflated. However, feedback recognizes the problem, but instead there is usually suggestions on ways to improve. I want to help you qualify what criticism is and how to deconstruct it, so you are not blindsided by it.

Have you ever had someone criticize something you say or do out of nowhere? Maybe you read a nasty comment on your social media. You can't stop thinking about what they wrote about you. No matter how hard you try, you lose focus and find yourself bothered by what they said, and you find yourself ruminating repeatedly on it. This used to be how I handled criticism. I used to spend hours, even days, being upset by a comment someone else made about me. Then I learned that there are effective ways to handle criticism. Don't get me wrong; I still have my moments when I feel the sting of criticism, but I am no longer paralyzed emotionally by what someone else has to say about me. I heard the saying recently, "Your perception of me is a reflection of you. My reaction to you is an awareness of me." I love this!

There are three things to remember about criticism:

1. Criticism is not always about you - There are some people who are miserable in their own life. They enjoy putting others down. The truth is it makes them feel good about themselves, and that's their sole reason for doing it. Perhaps you were just in the wrong place at the wrong time.
2. Criticism is inevitable - Remember that everyone has an opinion. This means that everybody's got something to say. If you are trying to improve yourself or your situation, get ready. This is when people close to you become the most critical. As mentioned earlier, everybody thinks they know how to run *your* life better than you do.

3. Decide if its criticism or feedback. If it's feedback, it may be justified. Try to use these 3 questions to determine your experience. Ask yourself:

- Who is giving their opinion to me? (Is it someone who doesn't even know me or who I really am?)
- How was it given? (Did the person try to build me up while explaining my short comings, or were their words vicious and mean?)
- Why was it given? (Was their view point given for my benefit or to personally attack me?)

Often what you need to hear the most is what you want to hear the least. Constructive feedback, if kept in perspective and with the right attitude, can be one of the fastest tools to help you grow as a person. Some of the best people who have helped me grow the most were not my friends but rather my critics. There is a saying, "If you are getting kicked in the behind, it's because you are upfront". The price of leadership is criticism. No one pays attention to last minute finishers. But when you're upfront, everything gets noticed.

> *"I've learned that you can't go through life with a catcher's mitt on both hands. You need to be able to throw something back."*
>
> ~ Maya Angelou

Feedback - how to give it to others

You want to always use empathy when giving someone feedback. It isn't always possible but try to compliment them first on something they did well before telling them the areas where they need improvement. This goes a long way and can make them want to do better. Try to put yourself in their shoes. How would you feel if your feedback was being given right back to you? Before you criticize anyone, you should always take the time to get your facts straight. Ask yourself, "Why am I finding fault with this person? What exactly do I want them to change?" Also, ask yourself if you genuinely feel that your feedback will make them better. Meaning, ask yourself if you are coming from a place of contribution.

You want to be careful not to address the person, but rather their actions. This is huge. Think of how you feel when someone is giving you feedback. Choose your words carefully. Remember, it's not what you say, it's how you say it. Try opening your statement with a phrase like "it seems to me..." or "l could be wrong, but....". These statements soften how its received and make it less likely that you are coming across as rude or arrogant. Lastly, focus on what can be done, not what has already been done. Keeping your feedback positive is important. Refer to specific areas that can be improved and avoid pointing out inadequacies.

There is nothing I hate more than when someone tries to criticize me for something that has already happened, and I can't do anything about it. Especially if they are chastising me for how I should have done the opposite thing. To me, that is not criticism, that is berating. For example, I invest in the stock market. If I made a bad trade and lost money, the last thing I need to hear from someone is how I should have done the opposite of that trade. Well, of course I should have. Hindsight is always 20/20. I feel like they are playing Monday morning quarterback. Tell me how I can improve my strategy, or tell me how to read the stock market charts better. Basically, tell me something that can be beneficial to me instead of making me feel bad about a decision that I cannot reverse or undo.

Think about my little example in the stock market when you are giving feedback to someone. How can you give them helpful information to make a better choice in the future? Telling someone how they messed up is not feedback, that's being a verbal bully. It's useless and will not win you points with them. Trust me!

Chapter Nineteen
Reach Back To Help Others

Let's talk

My mother had the biggest heart for helping other people. I've seen her buy food for single mothers. She trained dogs for people free of charge when they couldn't afford it. I've witnessed her on many occasions taking the limited resources that we had and giving it to a family that had even less than us. I wish I could tell you that, as a child, my heart was huge like hers. I want to tell you that I was a good example of a Christian girl, and that my mom and I were on the same page to save the world. However, I was a selfish child and did not hold to the values of any religion. Back then, I would get upset with her for giving money and food away when we didn't have much ourselves. She would always say, "God is watching, and He will provide for us." My mother never missed an opportunity to be kind. When she didn't have any financial resources to give, she would give her time by talking to people. She'd listen to their problems and pray over them. She'd make them laugh and cheer them up.

My mother had a true heart for God. Regardless of what your faith is, I want to share some uplifting words and love with you. I want to encourage you to share the goodness that is in your heart with others that you might come across.

Lessons learned

Now that I'm older and I've had many years to observe my own behavioral patterns, I see that I am very much like my mom. I have grown spiritually and realize that it is my obligation to look back and see how I can lift up someone else. I believe that to whom much is given, much is expected. I firmly believe that God blesses us so that we can be a blessing to others. It is not our job to hoard blessings for ourselves. We live in an abundant universe and the more you give to help others, the easier blessings will flow back into your life tenfold. I find that serving others is my greatest calling in life next to being a mother. Maybe you feel some version of this, too. Maybe there is a part of you that wants to serve others in some way, but perhaps you don't know where to begin.

No matter what our financial situation might be, there is always something that we each can give to help someone else. Whether it's a kind word, or a compliment, you can best believe that somebody would really appreciate hearing it from you. When you show love, you show God and your faith to the world. You may not realize it but we each hold within us the power to lift someone's mood in an instant. I remember one time I was having a rough morning. Some things were going on in my life that were overwhelming. That morning, I went for a walk and an older woman walked past and smiled at me as she said good morning. It was something about the way she smiled because I could feel the sincerity in her glance. A look of compassion and caring. I took a deep breath and felt gratitude. That woman had no idea what her smile and kind greeting did for me that day. It single handedly lifted my spirits and made me feel seen.

> "The smaller act of kindness is worth more than the grandest intention."
> ~ Oscar Wilde

Sow seeds in the lives of others

I have learned that people will try hard to rise to the level of your faith in them. When someone sees that you care enough to see the best in them, something comes alive inside their hearts. They want to make you proud, especially young people. I mentor young adults when and where I can. I'm not certified from a school or an organization, but I don't have to be to share guidance, kind words, or a prayer. I have two children who are older. My son has graduated college and is working full time. My daughter is still in college and navigating her way through. I have always made time for not only my own kids but also their friends. Even through high school, my kids' friends knew that they could count on me if they needed a listening ear. I do it because I genuinely love them. I feel honored that they share their struggles with me and entrust me to help guide them and give them advice. I believe that when you pour into the lives of other people's children, God will bless your kids as well.

On one particular night, I was about to turn out the lights and go to sleep when my phone lit up with a text from one of my daughter's friends. In fact, what makes this story extra special to me is that my daughter and her were in a season where their friendship had fallen to the wayside. They didn't talk regularly anymore, but this young lady knew I loved her and that I would still be there for her no matter what. She asked if we could FaceTime and I said sure. When I answered the FaceTime call, she burst into tears. She was having some issues she needed help with. She was struggling to make sense of things happening in her life. We talked for over an hour. I was able to help her see her situation with more clarity and less emotion. I reminded her how precious she is and how deserving of love she is. I walked her back to the part of herself that was strong and fearless and helped her to see how amazing she is. I reminded her how much God loves her. By the time the call ended, she was smiling and laughing with me. She told me that she didn't know what would have happened if I didn't answer her call.

Listen, I know that it might feel intimidating when it comes to helping others with an emotional or heart centered issue. I can see how that might seem daunting if you are not a therapist. You don't need to feel intimidated about helping others in this area because guess what? A good listener can serve the same purpose as a therapist if someone is hurting. You don't need to be qualified or have a prestigious degree to lend a loving heart to someone who may be struggling and just wants someone to help them feel heard.

The secret ingredient to being happy

If you look at where you are in life, chances are there is someone who helped you in some way to get where you are. Maybe someone put in a good recommendation for you to get the job you currently have. Maybe someone referred a client to you. Whatever it is, none of us can reach success completely alone. I encourage you to look around and see where and how you can make time to help someone else out. When you give, you are unlocking a part of God/source energy within you. When you meet somebody else's needs,

God will meet your needs. You are never more like God than when you are in the spirit of giving.

There are two types of people in this world. There are givers and there are takers. Trust me when I say that you will never be happy catering to yourself. Do you really want to get your happy back? One of the secret ingredients to being happy is to give, plain and simple. When you give your time or your resources to help someone else, you take the focus off your life and your problems. You are filled with something greater than yourself. Pay attention to those around you: your friends, coworkers, relatives, or even strangers. Some folks have a hard time asking for help, but you will see where there is a need if you just look around. I heard it said that you have not lived today until you have done something for someone who can never repay you. I have never felt more alive, happier, or filled with love than in the moments that I serve others, and I highly encourage you to help other humans where you can.

Principle #7
Get Your Happy Back

In this Principle, we will be discussing how to put yourself first and be intentional about your happiness and the life you deserve

- ♦ *Make your health a priority*

- ♦ *Happiness is intentional*

- ♦ *You've got this!*

LET'S GET STARTED!

Chapter Twenty
Make Your Health A Priority

Let's talk

It's hard to get your happy back if your physical body is not feeling good. One of the biggest culprits of feeling bad is putting the wrong foods in our bodies and expecting it to perform well. Food has energy just like everything else. Since we are energetic beings, we need to put foods that have the highest levels of energy in our bodies as often as possible. Fruits and vegetables have the highest levels of energy, and that's why they are the healthiest type of foods that we can eat. I am not a vegetarian, but I don't eat a lot of red meat. I am a chicken lover. I eat chicken at least three times a week. I also like turkey burgers. I do not eat a lot of fish due to the high levels of mercury and metals that can be found in them. The same is true for bottom feeder type seafood like lobster, shrimp, and crabs. I do eat these sometimes, but I limit them. You should do your own research about the damaging effects of mercury found in some seafood and what it does to our bodies. If you'd like to learn more about this, check out https://www.uofmhealth.org

    Our health is the one thing that is irreplaceable. Without our good health, we can find it hard to be happy with anything else in our life. Warren Buffet once gave an analogy that if someone gave you one automobile to last your entire lifetime, you'd probably make sure you changed the oil regularly. You'd also make sure that you took it in for service on time. You'd be sure that you took the very best care of it because you would need it to last your entire lifetime. Our bodies are no different. If you are not exercising, not eating healthy foods, consuming too much alcohol, not getting enough water or sleep; it will eventually catch up to you.

Lessons learned

The folks who know me well will tell you that I am always encouraging them to try green juicing. This is single handedly the best thing that I do for my health besides exercising. If you've never heard of it, there are two types of juicing. The first type of juicing is called "whole food" juicing, and this is where you put your fruits and veggies in a blender and you end up eating the whole smoothie mixture. This method is higher in fiber. The second type of juicing (which is the one I use) is called "juice extracting," and this involves a centrifugal-type juicer that extracts only the juices for consumption. I do this second method because you get more nutrients and less fiber. Some people like more fiber in their diet, but too much fiber doesn't always agree with my system.

It's personal preference. Both are excellent and serve for different health purposes. Research both methods to see which one is best for your health needs.

There are so many health benefits to juicing, and I have been doing it for years. I do it almost every day, except when I'm traveling. I have noticed that I have much more energy on the days that I do juicing than on the days when I don't. I cannot stress enough how much of an incredible health benefit juicing has been for me. I highly encourage you to investigate it for yourself.

Get to know your body

One of the best pieces of advice that I can give you when it comes to your health is to pay attention to your body. Start tracking certain data related to your health and mental wellbeing. Once you get enough data, you can start to see patterns. Track things like your water intake, the number hours of sleep you get and your moods, etc. These are just ideas of what types of things to track but get creative here. Figure out what kinds of data points you want to gather and start tracking them This is valuable information over a 30/60/90-day cycle. You will notice which days of the month you start to feel more irritable, brain fog, depressed or that feeling of a dark cloud hanging over you, etc. You can also correlate this to the number of hours of sleep that you are getting. For example, are you getting less sleep on the days leading up to an emotional meltdown, snapping at your kids or an argument with your partner? It's quite fascinating when you can step back and analyze data that is specific to your own life.

Get more sleep

I have always envied anyone who can fall asleep within seconds and are able to stay asleep all night, even with loud noises around them. I wish I could do that. I can't even remember the last time I was able to sleep all the way through the night. It was probably before I had kids. When my son was born, I would awaken at the slightest noise out of fear that he'd stop breathing. I was a nervous new mom. My kids are now grown, and it's still challenging to get a good night's rest. A high percentage of people suffer from lack of enough sleep. Maybe you are one of them. Everyone has different sleep cycles, and the amount of sleep we each need varies. For example, I need at least 8 hours, but there are people who can function fine on 4 or 5 hours of sleep. God bless them, but I need my 8 hours. The problem is that I haven't been getting it. My story is a work in progress, and I have made it my mission to get better results. They say that the only time your body can heal and rejuvenate is when it's in a deep sleep state. So, you can imagine how important it is for all of us to make getting enough sleep a priority. I am currently working on trying new and different things to get a better night's sleep. I will share with you some of the things that I am trying and if you need more sleep, maybe you can try these as well:

- No screen time or phone calls 30 mins before bed to quiet my mind
- Lighting candles to create a relaxing ambiance - but be sure to extinguish candle before you fall asleep. You don't want a fire to occur.
- Taking a hot bath to relax my body- this is probably one of my favorites
- Drink sleepy time tea
- Spend some time reading in bed
- Following a guided meditation using an app. I like to use www.Fragrantheart.com

Our sleep cycles are all different, so are the things that can help us sleep. For example, some people may find it hard to read before bed as it might get their mind too excited. Try a few of these to see what might work best for you.

> *Make yourself a priority. At the end of the day, you are your longest commitment.*
> ~ Anonymous

Mental and emotional health

Being healthy means more than just taking care of our physical body. We must tend to our spiritual, mental, and emotional health as well. Your mental state is such an important part of your day and your productivity. Not to mention, it is critical to being happy. You can't be happy if you are stressed out, worried, or anxious. Pay attention to what triggers your emotions. Is it a friend who always dumps their problems into your lap? A toxic partner who makes you question them and the relationship? Is it someone who makes you feel invaluable? I pay attention to how people make me feel when I'm around them and you should, too. Pay attention to your shifting energy. Your instincts will tell you. If someone is making you second guess your appearance, how smart you are, or how good you feel about yourself, you need to remove them from your life. They are not good for you. You should never have to change yourself to feel accepted or loved. Our relationships can be the greatest sources of our happiness or it can be the most painful experiences. We must learn to navigate these waters carefully. We will talk more about this area in the next chapter.

Protect your energy

There are certain times of day that we are most motivated, energetic, and highly productive. For me, it's first thing in the morning. I do whatever I can to protect this scared time. I'm going to share a tip that has helped me: I don't take any phone calls first thing in the morning. Unless it's one of my kids or an extremely close friend, that call will go to voice mail. Why? Because I know this is my time to set the intention for the rest of the day. This is when I do my morning routine that we talked about in an earlier chapter. This is when I am most energetic, mentally alert, and ready to tackle my goals. What time of day is this for you? You should treat this as your sacred time because you will need this valuable energy to get the most out of your day.

Saying no is a superpower

When it comes to getting your happy back, you must learn to say the word no. I always had a hard time saying no because I am a recovering people pleaser. A people pleaser is someone who wants everyone around them to be happy and will say yes to the needs of others, even to their own detriment. Who teaches us that we need to please others all the time anyways? What a croc, that it is. It's an important part of your emotional wellbeing and mental health to set proper boundaries and stand up for your happiness. I realize that, like me, saying no may be hard for you. So try this: when someone asks you to commit to something and you're unsure if you want to do it but don't feel comfortable saying no on the spot, make your default response something like, "Let me think about it, and I'll get back to you." Another tip that has helped me in protecting my mental peace is that I try not to answer my phone calls directly anymore. If I am in a happy mental state, one phone call can change or disrupt it. The person on the other end might mean well, but they could also be in a bad mood and say something that is argumentative, condescending, or negative. Maybe they don't mean it, but people are people. You can always call them back when you are in a better mental space and prepared to take their call. Your happy mental state is a valuable commodity. When you are enjoying it and vibing with yourself, don't let others swoop in to steal it from you. You get to decide when someone has access to you, not the other way around.

Chapter Twenty-One

Happiness Is Intentional

Let's talk

I have always wanted the people around me to be happy. I think I inherited this trait from my mother, who went out of her way to help others. It wasn't until a few years ago that I started to become consciously aware that that the harder I tried to please everyone, the more my own happiness suffered. It also became apparent that no matter how hard I tried, I could not make certain people happy. I came to two realizations: (1.) some people enjoy drama, and (2.) I needed to prioritize my own happiness. While it may be hard for you to comprehend this, there are people among us who get an emotional fix by having their life in a constant state of chaos. They like the attention their perpetual dilemmas bring. Then they wonder why their lives are not prosperous, why they don't have healthy relationships, and why they feel sad often. I've seen it with my own eyes and actually had to end a friendship over this toxic behavior.

A while back, I met a woman who I came to know through mutual interests. I don't let many people into my inner circle, but over time, it seemed as if we were slowly becoming friends. We didn't hang out regularly, but when we did connect, it was easy to pick up where we left off.

Our friendship flourished as we shared our compatibilities ranging from stories about our kids, the challenges of dating over 40, to career and financial decisions. We were close, or so I thought. One day, she unexpectedly erupted over something very trivial. I was shocked by her intense anger and the mean words she began to text me. I was also completely blindsided by her bizarre behavior and at a loss for how to handle the situation as this had never happened to me before. Instead of my initial inclination to stand up for myself against her attack, I was actually worried and concerned for her. I tried to be the voice of reason to calm her but the more I tried to understand why she was so upset, her remarks became even more offensive and abusive.

Something didn't feel right about this situation or our friendship at this point. In a normal disagreement between two friends, there should be an element of grace, forgiveness or an opportunity to make things right. I took a few minutes to ponder, and then it hit me. Early in our friendship she bragged how she could easily turn on a dime when upset and that a few long term friends had stopped speaking to her over this. She was very animated and always made me laugh so I thought she was joking. However, now that I was on the receiving end of her attack, I realized those stories weren't embellished at all. She really had a dark side.

It became obvious that she didn't want a resolution. What she wanted was to continue to berate me, and for me to sit there and take it. Moreover, she wanted to show that she was in control of the dynamics of our friendship, and at any time she could turn the tides if things didn't go her way. I learned a lot that day.

Lessons learned

Oprah Winfrey said it best, "When someone shows you who they are believe them." I ended our friendship that day and blocked her. I was deeply hurt that someone that I adored and trusted could turn on a dime and be so mean and cruel for no good reason.

I did nothing to deserve the wrath that she forced upon me. In fact, she and I were getting along great just an hour earlier, which made it even more bizarre, hurtful, and confusing. But here's what you need to know about abusers: if they've done it to others, they will do it to you. She came across as such a sweet and loving person. However, when she shared how she had treated former friends, I should have paid closer attention. That was not normal behavior. How someone treats their former boss/coworkers, previous spouse, or friends is how they can treat you. Read that again!

For the record, I forgave her and do not hold any grudges. However, I cannot allow someone like this to stay in my life, and neither should you. Once someone shows you who they are, you must act accordingly. To be clear, I am not referring to the behaviors of someone who is having a bad day. I am talking about vicious verbal and emotional abuse. The kind that shocks you to your core. Often we think that we are obligated to accept verbal abuse because it can be disguised as someone venting their feelings or being in a bad mood. No more of that nonsense. You must learn that when someone's behavior or words make you feel small, attacked or bullied, that is not okay. Not ever. This rule applies to even the closest people in your life including your spouse, family, and friends.

Listen, it's not easy to end a friendship or a relationship with someone that you love or care about. However, you need to cut some people out of your life for your own peace of mind. You need to understand that their issues are not your issues. There is a right and wrong way for us to relate to one another as humans. If someone is being abusive, they need to be given a one-way ticket out of your life.

> "The power of intention is the power to manifest, to create, to live a life of unlimited abundance, and to attract into your life the right people at the right moments."
>
> ~ Dr. Wayne Dyer

Stay in peace

The reason I am sharing this story with you is that you could be the kindest and most giving person, and then out of nowhere something throws you off your horse. Like me, you could be blindsided by the betrayal of a friend, the discovery of an unfaithful partner, or a health issue that leaves you shaken. These events can be jolting and devastating. However, I want you to know that you can have peace during any storm. If you base your inner peace on your circumstances, you will be sorely disappointed because there will always be something to upset you. I want you to learn the importance of having a base reference point of inner peace as a daily practice. This is known as your *emotional home*. This is the level of happiness you naturally migrate back to based on what you believe about yourself. When you have a healthy emotional home for yourself, you are less likely to allow someone to pull you from it and thrust you into their chaos. When crazy comes knocking, you will be able to process things from a better perspective. By the way, if your emotional home needs a makeover, meaning you want to increase this level of protection for yourself, you must practice more self-love. Everything in your life gets better when you increase your self-esteem.

This means knowing your value and understanding that you are worthy and deserving of love and happiness. When you know your true worth, you are less likely to take things personally. If something tries to steal your joy, you will be better equipped to immediately shut it down and get back to your peaceful emotional state. I heard a quote, "Don't use your faith to try to get rid of all your problems. Use your faith to remain calm in the midst of your problems." I love this because it sums up this chapter perfectly. You can be in the storm, but don't let the storm get inside of you. Sometimes we lose our peace over things we can't control, but we must learn to walk above the circumstances. Remain in a state of love, forgiveness, and peace for others, while implementing healthy and strong boundaries for yourself. This is what being intentional about your happiness is all about!

The power of gratitude

Robert Emmons, a Professor of Psychology at the University of California, conducted a study to determine from a scientific perspective if it was possible to make people more grateful. One of the key methods he used for this was to have people keep a gratitude journal. They had to write down something they were grateful for 3-4 times per week for three weeks. His research found that by doing this simple act, it created a meaningful difference in one's levels of happiness. Some of the reasons this is so effective is:

1. It brings us into the present - It forces us to focus on what's right in front of us. There's no need for feeling angst or regret about things that happened in the past.

Today is a new day and there are many things to be thankful for if we open our eyes and choose to see them.
2. It reminds us of how we are all connected as human beings - With today's technology, it's becoming easier to have little physical contact with each other with the use of cell phones, email, the internet, video conferencing, telecommuting, etc., so taking the time to write down who touched our life that day and why we are thankful for them, keeps us connected and reminds us that we are not alone.
3. It forces us to focus on what went right in our day - so often we tend to focus and complain to our friends when something goes wrong. The good barely gets mentioned. By writing in our gratitude journal about only the things that we are thankful for, it's like we are giving life to the positive things in our world by allowing ourselves to see them.
4. It increases our self-esteem. Isn't it wonderful to remind ourselves how good things have happened to us? Subconsciously, we tell ourselves that we are worth it, and that good things do happen to good people.

Having a sense of gratitude in everything that happens to us changes our perspective on life. Therefore, it's important to remember what we are thankful for. Keeping a gratitude journal is a great way to remember our daily run-ins with happiness. When we write something down, even if we already know it, it helps us to be more intentional and present.

Chapter Twenty-Two
You've Got This!

Let's talk

I know that if you are reading this book, chances are life has kicked you around. Maybe life has even thrown you a curve ball or two like the ones I shared in my story. It's so easy to get discouraged in life, especially if you feel like you've had a disadvantage right out of the gate. In a perfect world, we would all have two loving parents, a fun-filled childhood and a loving family to support and guide us through life. However, we live in a broken world. People mean well, but they are fallible, hurt, and broken themselves. Sometimes they are doing their best just to fumble their way through. We learn that people can't give us what they don't have.

When I think back on everything I've been able to overcome, I can't help but think of the season that came beforehand. That season of heartbreak, that season of loneliness, despair, and pain. That season of uncertainty and not knowing how things were going to turn out. That season of darkness that was all around me, and the only light I could see was God's promise to give us beauty for ashes. I know that you may have had some of these scary seasons in your life. Maybe you are going through a season right now. I want to share with you that it's in these times of hardship that your warrior spirit is born. You have the heart of a fighter, and you need to summon this inner strength to keep going even when you want to give up.

Let me be candid about something here: I've spent my entire life fighting. Fighting to overcome the rejection of my father whose love I desperately wanted but never got. Fighting to put myself through college and then build a new life after my divorce and the death of my mom who was my everything.

I didn't ask to be a fighter. In fact, I really don't like being in battles at all and I find it extremely exhausting. But do you know what the defining difference is? I keep showing up for myself. And that is what I want for you.

And if we're being honest, I know I have a fighting spirit inside of me whether I consider myself a fighter or not. She will kick your butt and mine, too, if necessary. You've got this same ferocious fighting spirit inside of you. It's in there, ready to help you when needed. You have to learn that it's okay to call on it.

Maybe you've had to dig and claw to pave your own way, and that's okay. It has made you who you are today. Don't ever allow someone, or even yourself, to make you feel less than because of your struggles. You should embrace and be proud of what you have been able to overcome. You are still standing. You are still here and fighting for a better way. There is a bright future out there for the taking. The mere fact that you have read this book means that you are determined to make things better in your life. Deep down inside, you know what's possible for you. I am here to tell you that you *can* and *will* rise above any of your circumstances if you are willing to roll up your sleeves and put in the work. When we look at our life, we will either find excuses or opportunities. I want you to make it your resolve to look around your life and find every opportunity to be your own hero. *You* get to decide what your next chapter will look like.

Lessons learned

Don't lose your fire! People lose their passion for life when they are not actively pursuing something they care about. Refuse to give up on the dreams in your heart.

Keep moving. Keep looking for challenges. It is unhealthy to not pursue something each day. Everything may not be perfect in your life, but if you don't learn to be happy where you are now, you will never get to where you want to be.

My goal for writing this book was to look back over my journey and pull out the most important principles that have really helped me to overcome the big obstacles. More importantly, they have helped me stay hopeful and happy about life. My prayer is that these principles will also do the same for you.

I'm excited for you to:

- **Principle 1 - *Turn your past into your power*** - Let go of your past or at least reframe it so it can serve you. Meaning pull out all the good that came from those bad experiences. How did it shape you? Who did you become because of those hard times?
- **Principle 2 - *Expand your awareness*** - Learn to practice self-love every day by keeping small promises to yourself. Take the time to learn your core values so that you can start making decisions that are congruent with them.
- **Principle 3 - *Create your mental tool kit*** - Keep fresh new goals in front of you. Develop a strong mindset and use the power of visualization to manifest the amazing things in your life that you deserve.
- **Principle 4 - *Form amazing habits*** - Implement a powerful morning routine to help set the tone for each

day and start establishing small habits to help you achieve your goals faster!
- *Principle 5 - Learn to pivot* - Dare to dream about the life you really want to have. Get curious about what lights you up from the inside. Reinvent yourself and be open to discovering what's truly possible for you when you put in the effort.
- *Principle 6 - Level up* - Surround yourself with positive people in person or online who can inspire you and lift you up. Stop playing small and look for what you can do to help others.
- *Principle 7 - Get your happy back* - Learn to put yourself first for a change. Your physical, mental, and emotional health and happiness are your greatest assets, and you must do what's necessary to preserve and protect them. Life will never be perfect, but the key is to find happiness in each day. Keep showing up, you've got this!

> *"Courage is not having the strength to go on; it's going on when you don't have the strength."*
> ~ Theodore Roosevelt

Make your move!

The one big takeaway that I want you to get from this book is that you are powerful! More powerful than you realize. You can shift your entire life with just one thought. That thought might sound something like:

- I'm not happy in my career, and I want to explore options to change it.
- I'm not happy in my marriage or relationship, and I've made the decision to renegotiate things or end it.

- I'm tired of being a doormat to my family and friends, so I'm making myself and my needs a priority by setting some boundaries from here on.
- I'm fed up with being out of shape and overweight. I'm joining a gym today and will commit to new daily healthy habits.
- I thought I'd be further ahead in my life than where I am, so I'm making the decision today to set some new financial goals for myself to prepare for a better future.

These thoughts will create a momentum in your life to get the ball rolling. Make your move while you're still on fire from this book! When you do, you will eventually see significant results. You need to prove to yourself that you can do this. If you start to feel nervous or scared at the thought of making changes in your life, you are not alone. I was scared to make every single change, and here's what you need to know: I did it anyway, and you will too. Courage pays off, fear does not. No one is going to come along and fix your life for you. Stop tolerating people and situations in your life that make you overanalyze everything. Stop settling for not having enough money for travel and the fun things you want to do in this life. Stop the negative self-talk. Stop doing unhealthy things to cope with situations that you know you must address head on. I challenge you to get a hold of your life. Get free from your past thats been haunting you. Get scared but do it anyway. Get the courage to get your happy back!

About the Author

From being homeless as a kid to owning millions of dollars in real estate, Diamond Leone has been dubbed the "Comeback Queen." No matter how big the setback, she knows a thing or two about pulling yourself up by the bootstraps and creating the life you deserve, all while maintaining her sense of humor throughout the hardships! She has spent years studying the science of personal achievement and why some people are successful and happy, and why others are not.

Frequently drawing on experiences from her own life, she can easily connect with and reach people of all ages, socioeconomic backgrounds, and belief systems. She has the extraordinary ability to hear what's not being said when someone is struggling and the gift to deliver strategies and guidance that move the needle for success and happiness.

Today, her life's mission is to make the world a better place by helping others understand the importance of self-love, how to find happiness from within, and empowers others to reach their full potential in their relationships, their work, and their communities. She has instilled these important principles in her own children over the years, their friends, and countless other young adults that she has mentored.

She is the mother of two amazing kids, the best Auntie ever, and the fun friend you didn't know you needed. She loves to praise the Lord, laugh & dance, and values time with family. She resides in Palm Beach, FL.

Diamond is the host of the "Get Your Happy Back" Podcast and you can find her on most social media platforms:

Instagram @TheDiamondLeone
Youtube @DiamondLeone
Tik Tok @DiamondLeone
Twitter @DiamondLeone
LinkedIn @DiamondLeone

www.ingramcontent.com/pod-product-compliance
Lightning Source LLC
Chambersburg PA
CBHW031248290426
44109CB00012B/486